BIRDING MISSOURI
A GUIDE TO SEASONAL HIGHLIGHTS

Other books from Willow Press:

Hiking Ohio, Scenic Trails of the Buckeye State
Hiking Kentucky, Scenic Trails of the Bluegrass State
Walking the Denver-Boulder Region
Hiking Mid-Missouri, Scenic Trails of the Heartland
A Birder's Guide to the Cincinnati Tristate
Birding the Front Range, A Guide to Seasonal Highlights
Colorado's Year, A Guide to Nature's Highlights
A Guide to American Zoos & Aquariums

About the Author:

Robert Folzenlogen is a physician and naturalist who has written a number of outdoor guides, including those listed above. All of his books are dedicated to the themes of open space protection, historic preservation and wildlife conservation.

Cover Photo:

Great Horned Owl, a permanent resident of Missouri. Photo by Sherm Spoelstra

BIRDING MISSOURI
A GUIDE TO SEASONAL HIGHLIGHTS

by Robert Folzenlogen

Willow Press
Columbia, Missouri
Littleton, Colorado

ISBN: 1-893111-02-4
Library of Congress Control Number: 2001098988

Published by: **Willow Press**
                 Columbia, Missouri
                 Littleton, Colorado
                 Email: willowpress@eudoramail.com

Printed by: John S. Swift Co., Inc.
                 Cincinnati, Ohio

Cover and interior bird photos by:

          Sherm Spoelstra
          Highlands Ranch, Colorado

Landscape photos and maps by author

For Darcy, Sarah, Zach and Ally

Acknowledgements

This guide blends my own research with information provided by many conservation organizations and nature preserves throughout Missouri. Their contributions are acknowledged in the Appendix and Bibliography of this book and their dedication to the protection of natural habitat is vital to all of us who care about wildlife conservation. Our opportunity to explore wild spaces and to observe wild creatures depends, in large part, on the vigilance of these organizations. Your active participation and financial support are strongly encouraged.

My thanks to Jan Jolley and her associates at the John S. Swift Company for their technical assistance and to Sherm Spoelstra, whose bird photos grace this book.

Finally, my love and thanks to Darcy, Sarah, Zach and Ally for their understanding and encouragement.

- Robert Folzenlogen

CONTENTS

American White Pelicans   (photo by Sherm   Spoelstra)

INTRODUCTION

Beginning birdwatchers, and those visiting a new area, want to know where to go, when to go there and what birds they might expect to find. This guide is designed to provide that information, placing emphasis on the natural habitats of Missouri and on the seasonal fluctuation of regional bird populations.

Chapter I introduces the reader to the landscape of Missouri, describing the geophysical regions of our State, while **Chapter II** provides an overview of the component habitats. A bird list, grouped by season, is offered for each habitat. Backyard birding is also discussed in this chapter.

Chapter III takes the birder through Missouri's year, directing him/her to seasonal birdwatching highlights. Twenty-five areas are included, chosen to highlight the varied habitats of the State. Each area is illustrated with maps and photos and specific directions from regional cities or highways is provided.

Finally, **Chapter IV** is a checklist of Missouri's birds; **316 species** are included in the list. For each species, the guide indicates that bird's seasonal occurance in Missouri, describes its preferred habitat and recommends a site and season for observing the bird.

The **Appendix** lists Missouri Conservation Organizations that are working to protect our natural areas; your support for their efforts is strongly encouraged. A **Bibliography** (books, bird lists and websites) and an **Index** complete the guide.

BIRDING EQUIPMENT

Fortunately, birdwatching is an inexpensive hobby. Nevertheless, some basic equipment is recommended.

This book does not illustrate the various bird species; beginning birders are encouraged to obtain one of the Field Guides recommended in the Bibliography. A good pair of binoculars is essential and adventurous birdwatchers are advised to bring sunscreen, layered clothing, insect repellent and sturdy, waterproof hiking boots. Though not essential, a good spotting scope will come in handy when observing distant flocks of waterfowl, shorebirds and grassland species.

WHEN TO GO BIRDING

Birds, like most mammals, tend to be most active during the early morning and late daylight hours; it is thus most productive to plan your birding excursions for those times of the day. Be sure to visit your local parks and nature preserves during each season of the year; beginning birders often confine their field trips to the warmer months, thereby missing the winter residents and visitors. Since wildlife is best observed during quiet walks through natural areas, plan your field trips on weekdays and visit popular parks during the "off-season" months of the year.

THE ART OF BIRDWATCHING

Before heading out to the parks and nature preserves, familiarize yourself with the common backyard birds and look through a Field Guide to gain a general understanding of the various bird families. This will make your field trips more enjoyable and productive. When visiting an area recommended in this guide, read through the chapter before your trip, learning what species you might expect to see; then review their identifying features before the trip.

As mentioned above, birds are best observed during the early morning or late daylight hours; a few species, such as owls, nightjars and woodcocks, are best observed at dusk. Plan an unhurried walk through a variety of natural habitats, stopping frequently to let the wildlife adjust to your presence. Seasoned birders often use soft "pishing" noises to bring inquisitive songbirds into view.

Birdwatching from the car also has certain advantages. Not only are you protected from inclement weather but the car serves as a blind, allowing you to approach birds that might otherwise flee your presence. This is especially helpful when visiting wetlands that are accessed by gravel roads; shorebirds, waders and waterfowl can often be viewed at close range.

Most importantly, respect our nature preserves by staying on designated trails and by leaving the native flora undisturbed. Always view wildlife from a safe and nonthreatening distance. Pack out any garbage that you may produce during your visit and pick up any that you encounter along the trail. Always respect private boundaries and, for your own protection, become familiar with local hunting laws and dates. Finally, help to protect our open spaces by donating time and/or money to the Conservation Organizations listed in the Appendix.

- Robert Folzenlogen

KEY TO THE MAPS

ROADS:

PARKING AREAS:

TRAILS/LEVEES:

LAKES/STREAMS:

MARSH/WETLAND:

WOODLANDS:

CLIFFS:

4

I. THE LANDSCAPE OF MISSOURI

Missouri encompasses four primary geologic provinces: the Glaciated Plain, the Osage Plain, the Ozark Plateau and the Gulf Coastal Plain. In addition, the Ozark Borderlands and the Missouri-Mississippi Floodplains augment the natural diversity.

Glaciated Plain. Most of the land north of the Missouri River falls within this province. Scoured and enriched by Pleistocene glaciers, this relatively flat landscape is characterized by fertile soil and was once covered by a vast tallgrass prairie. Most of this natural grassland has since succumbed to the farmer's plow and is now part of the American Corn Belt. Woodlands are relatively sparse and, where they occur, are clustered along the primary drainages. Most streams flow southward to join the Missouri River; an exception is the Salt River watershed of northeast Missouri which drains eastward into the Mississippi River. Man-made reservoirs now dot the Glaciated Plains, attracting huge flocks of migratory waterfowl.

Osage Plain. Covering western Missouri (see map), this province was also covered by tallgrass prairie before modern settlers arrived. Unglaciated, this prairie land was maintained by periodic wildfires, by relatively thin, dry soil and by the grazing of huge bison herds. Parcels of the magnificent prairie still cover limited areas of western Missouri though much of the Osage Plain has been ranched and "developed." Upland sandpipers and greater prairie chickens still haunt the prairie remnants and new backwater wetlands, created by man-made reservoirs, add to the region's diversity. As in the Glaciated Plains, woodlands are primarily confined to the stream channels, all of which empty toward the Missouri River.

Tallgrass prairie at Prairie State Park

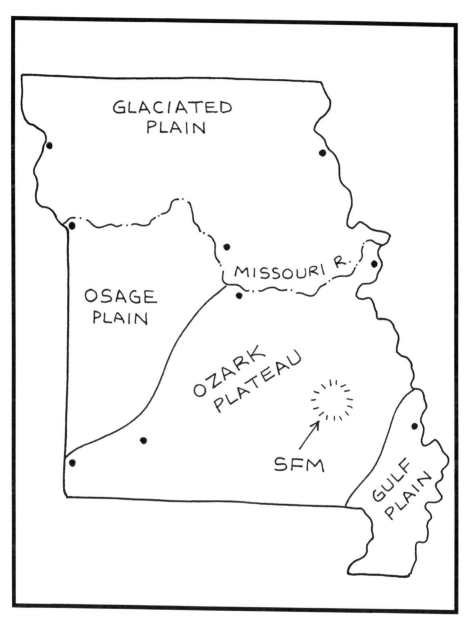

GLACIATED
PLAIN

OSAGE
PLAIN

MISSOURI R.

OZARK
PLATEAU

SFM

GULF
PLAIN

GEOLOGIC PROVINCES OF MISSOURI

Ozark Plateau. This broad uplift of horizontal, early Paleozoic sediments, covers most of the southern half of Missouri. Extending into northern Arkansas, the plateau has been carved into a maze of ridges and valleys by the tributaries of the Missouri and Arkansas Rivers. Near the eastern end of the Ozark Plateau, a domal uplift of Precambrian rock has been sculpted into the St. Francois Mountains, the highest elevations in the State.

Almost all of the Ozark Plateau was once covered by a vast forest of oak, hickory and pine. Timber production, farming and strip mining have taken their toll on this ecosystem but large tracts of forest are now protected within wilderness areas, State Forests and the Mark Twain National Forest. Black bear still patrol the woods and wild turkeys have made a dramatic comeback. Even a few mountain lions may still roam the plateau.

The hilly terrain of south-central and east-central Missouri represents a transition zone from the Ozark Plateau to the Glaciated Plains. Further bisected by the broad floodplain of the Missouri River, this region was a mosaic of forest, open woodlands and meadows before man plowed and paved most of it. Columbia and Jefferson City lie within this border zone.

Gulf Coastal Plain. Missouri's Bootheel and a swath to its north were covered by an arm of the Gulf of Mexico through much of the late Mesozoic and Cenozoic Eras. Now a fertile lowland of floodplain woods, cypress swamps and oxbow lakes, the region boasts a tremendous diversity of wildlife. Huge flocks of waterfowl winter in the region and Mississippi kites are among the summer residents. Rice fields now dot the area, attracting a wide variety of waders and shorebirds.

Missouri and Mississippi Floodplains. As the last Pleistocene glacier receeded into Canada, some 10,000 years ago, a tremendous volume of meltwater was carried by the North American rivers. The broad floodplains of the Missouri and Mississippi Rivers were molded during this time and have since been widened by periodic floods and by relentless erosion along their banks. Today, the rivers and their associated wetlands offer migratory highways and reststops for waterfowl, shorebirds, ospreys, and water birds of all kinds. Migrant songbirds also follow these broad valleys and the riverside woodlands fill with warblers, flycatchers, vireos and orioles during the spring and fall.

Upland forest of the Ozark Plateau

Swamp forest at Otter Slough in southeast Missouri

II. THE NATURAL HABITATS OF MISSOURI

The geophysical provinces discussed in Chapter I are, themselves, made up of component habitats. This Chapter presents the basic natural habitats that characterize the Missouri landscape. A bird list is provided for each habitat, grouping those species by seasonal occurance. Since birds are highly mobile creatures, many species are included in more than one habitat.

Beginning birdwatchers soon learn that the variety of birds found in a nature preserve will be directly proportional to the diversity of habitat in that refuge.

DEEP LAKES & RIVERS. This habitat occurs along the Missouri and Mississippi Rivers and across the deeper waters of the State's lakes and reservoirs. It is favored by birds that fish from above (eagles and ospreys) and by those birds that dive from the surface (loons, cormorants and diving ducks).

PERMANENT RESIDENTS

hooded merganser

SUMMER RESIDENTS & VISITORS

anhinga	double-crested cormorant	least tern

WINTER RESIDENTS & VISITORS

common loon	canvasback	redhead
lesser scaup	common goldeneye	bufflehead
ring-necked duck	white-winged scoter	black scoter
oldsquaw	common merganser	herring gull
ring-billed gull	common black-headed gull	glaucous gull
Thayer's gull	lesser black-backed gull	gr black-backed gull
bald eagle		

*Smithville Lake is a great place to find loons,
grebes and diving ducks*

MIGRANTS

common loon	yellow-billed loon	pacific loon
red-throated loon	Clark's grebe	western grebe
red-necked grebe	horned grebe	eared grebe
double-cr. cormorant	ruddy duck	osprey
redhead	greater scaup	lesser scaup
black scoter	white-winged scoter	surf scoter
oldsquaw	red-breasted merganser	Franklin's gull
Bonaparte's gull	common tern	Forster's tern
black tern	Caspian tern	

LAKE SHALLOWS & WETLANDS. This habitat occurs along the shoreline of lakes, in the reservoir backwaters and in marshlands across the State. It is the domain of surface-feeding waterfowl, waders, shorebirds and rails.

PERMANENT RESIDENTS

great blue heron	Canada goose	mallard
wood duck	pied-billed grebe	American coot
northern shoveler	red-winged blackbird	song sparrow

SUMMER RESIDENTS & VISITORS

least bittern	American bittern	black-cr night heron
green-backed heron	yellow-cr night heron	little blue heron
snowy egret	great egret	glossy ibis
white ibis	white-faced ibis	roseate spoonbill
blue-winged teal	Virginia rail	king rail
sora	common moorhen	spotted sandpiper
black-necked stilt	killdeer	com. yellowthroat
marsh wren	sedge wren	great-tailed grackle
savannah sparrow	yellow-headed blackbird	

WINTER RESIDENTS & VISITORS

snow goose	American black duck	gadwall
green-winged teal	northern pintail	common snipe
peregrine falcon	Lincoln's sparrow	swamp sparrow

MIGRANTS

Am. white pelican	white-faced ibis	sandhill crane
tundra swan	trumpeter swan	greater w-fr goose
snow goose	Ross' goose	brant
Am. wigeon	gadwall	northern pintail
northern shoveler	cinnamon teal	yellow rail
black rail	American avocet	black-necked stilt
snowy plover	semipalmated plover	piping plover
black-bellied plover	lesser golden plover	marbled godwit
Hudsonian godwit	whimbrel	long-billed curlew
willet	greater yellowlegs	lesser yellowlegs
solitary sandpiper	red-necked phalarope	Wilson's phalarope

(list continued next page)

short-b. dowitcher
common snipe
dunlin
western sandpiper
Baird's sandpiper
LeConte's sparrow

long-billed dowitcher
ruddy turnstone
semipalmated sandpiper
white-rumped sandpiper
pectoral sandpiper
sharp-tailed sparrow

stilt sandpiper
red knot
sanderling
least sandpiper
palm warbler

Shallow wetlands at Eagle Bluffs

RIPARIAN WOODLANDS. This term refers to woodlands along streams, marshlands and lakeshores. Certain raptors, kingfishers, swallows, woodpeckers and water-loving songbirds characterize the bird population.

PERMANENT RESIDENTS

red-shouldered hawk red-headed woodpecker belted kingfisher
barred owl

SUMMER RESIDENTS & VISITORS

Amerian woodcock Mississippi kite summer tanager
black-billed cuckoo yellow-billed cuckoo eastern kingbird
alder flycatcher yellow-bellied flycatcher tree swallow
fish crow blue-gray gnatcatcher Bell's vireo
prothonotary warbler cerulean warbler yellow-thr. warbler
yellow warbler northern oriole

WINTER RESIDENTS & VISITORS

winter wren American tree sparrow rusty blackbird

MIGRANTS

veery Philadelphia vireo mourning warbler
Wilson's warbler Swainson's warbler n. waterthrush

*Riparian
woodlands*

A woodland glade at the Henning C.A.

IMMATURE WOODLANDS & THICKETS. This habitat is composed of young trees, shrubs, thickets and hedgerows. Characteristic birds include wrens, goldfinches, hummingbirds, cardinals, certain warblers and some species of sparrow.

PERMANENT RESIDENTS

Carolina wren	Bewick's wren	American robin
northern mockingbird	brown thrasher	cedar waxwing
northern cardinal	rufous-sided towhee	song sparrow
house sparrow	Eurasian sparrow	American goldfinch
house finch		

SUMMER RESIDENTS & VISITORS

house wren	ruby-throated hummingbird	blue-gr. gnatcatcher
gray catbird	white-eyed vireo	blue-winged warbler
yellow-br. chat	golden-winged warbler	American redstart
blue grosbeak	indigo bunting	painted bunting

WINTER RESIDENTS & VISITORS

Bohemian waxwing	American tree sparrow	dark-eyed junco
white-thr. sparrow	fox sparrow	common redpoll

MIGRANTS

Swainson's thrush	orange-crowned warbler	Nashville warbler

OPEN WOODLANDS. This habitat is typical of wooded meadows, glades, savannahs and suburban areas. Bluebirds, certain woodpeckers, blue jays, siskins, some flycatchers, wild turkeys and sharp-shinned hawks typify the bird population.

PERMANENT RESIDENTS

Cooper's hawk	wild turkey	northern bobwhite
common grackle	red-bellied woodpecker	northern flicker
blue jay	black-capped chickadee	Carolina chickadee
white-br. nuthatch	red-breasted nuthatch	house finch
downy woodpecker	hairy woodpecker	eastern bluebird
loggerhead shrike	northern mockingbird	cedar waxwing
European starling	brown-headed cowbird	field sparrow
pine warbler		

SUMMER RESIDENTS & VISITORS

whip-poor-will	Chuck-will's-widow	common nighthawk
chimney swift	ruby-throated hummingbird	eastern phoebe
olive-sid. flycatcher	great-crested flycatcher	least flycatcher
willow flycatcher	tree swallow	golden-cr. kinglet
warbling vireo	northern parula	prairie warbler
rose-br. grosbeak	indigo bunting	Bachman's sparrow
chipping sparrow	dickcissel	orchard oriole
northern oriole	summer tanager	

WINTER RESIDENTS & VISITORS

sharp-shinned hawk	northern goshawk	merlin
northern shrike	yellow-rumped warbler	Bohemain waxwing
Harris' sparrow	white-crowned sparrow	pine siskin
red crossbill	white-winged crossbill	brown creeper
purple finch	evening grosbeak	

MIGRANTS

ruby-crowned kinglet	solitary vireo	Tennessee warbler
chestnut-sid. warbler	cape may warbler	magnolia warbler
blackpoll warbler	black-thr. green warbler	bay-br. warbler
clay-colored sparrow		

Open woods along Stockton Lake

Oak Savannah at Ha Ha Tonka State Park

MATURE FOREST & WOODLOTS. This habitat includes the large, mature trees and a well-developed understory. Characteristic birds include broad-winged hawks, certain owls, pileated woodpeckers, thrushes, vireos, and many warblers.

PERMANENT RESIDENTS

great horned owl
downy woodpecker
Carolina chickadee

eastern screech owl
pileated woodpecker
black-capped chickadee

hairy woodpecker
tufted titmouse
white-br. nuthatch

SUMMER RESIDENTS & VISITORS

broad-winged hawk
wood thrush
Kentucky warbler
L. waterthrush
scarlet tanager

eastern wood pewee
yellow-throated vireo
black & white warbler
worm-eating warbler

acadian flycatcher
red-eyed vireo
hooded warbler
ovenbird

WINTER RESIDENTS & VISITORS

northern goshawk
brown creeper
hermit thrush
fox sparrow

northern saw-whet owl
yellow-bellied sapsucker
yellow-rumped warbler

long-eared owl
golden-cr. kinglet
red-br. nuthatch

MIGRANTS

gray-cheeked thrush
Canada warbler

black-thr. blue warbler

Blackburn. warbler

Crossing the swamp forest at Big Oak Tree State Park

Winter Woods

GRASSLANDS. This habitat includes prairie remnants, fields, meadows and farmlands. Meadowlarks, most hawks, vultures, horned larks, long-spurs, short-eared owls, many sparrows and snow buntings are among the typical bird species.

PERMANENT RESIDENTS

turkey vulture
American kestrel
common grackle
rock dove
horned lark
American robin
field sparrow
Eurasian sparrow

northern harrier
greater prairie chicken
ring-necked pheasant
greater roadrunner
red-winged blackbird
loggerhead shrike
eastern meadowlark
house sparrow

red-tailed hawk
northern bobwhite
mourning dove
barn owl
eastern bluebird
European starling
American crow

SUMMER RESIDENTS & VISITORS

cattle egret
Mississippi kite
barn swallow
sedge wren
vesper sparrow
dickcissel

upland sandpiper
Swainson's hawk
scissor-tailed flycatcher
grasshopper sparrow
savannah sparrow
great-tailed grackle

black vulture
western kingbird
purple martin
Henslow's sparrow
lark sparrow
bobolink

WINTER RESIDENTS & VISITORS

snow goose
short-eared owl
American pipit
snow bunting

rough-legged hawk
snowy owl
Lapland longspur
western meadowlark

prairie falcon
northern shrike
Smith's longspur
Brewer's blackbird

MIGRANTS

snow goose
sandhill crane
buff-br sandpiper
bobolink

greater white-fr. goose
long-billed curlew
Franklin's gull

brant
pectoral sandpiper
lesser golden plover

Taberville   Prairie

A woodland meadow at Lake of the Ozarks State Park

BACKYARD BIRDING. The variety of birds in your backyard will depend, in part, on your efforts to attract them. Berry producing shrubs entice cardinals, cedar waxwings, robins and orioles while conifers attract pine siskins, red-breasted nuthatches and evening grosbeaks. Nectar rich flowers draw hummingbirds and brush piles bring wrens, thrashers, juncos and a variety of sparrows to your yard.

   Feeders are also important. Sunflower seed is a magnet for cardinals, blue jays, titmice, chickadees, and nuthatches while Niger (thistle) brings in goldfinches, siskins, house finches and purple finches; juncos, mourning doves and white-throated sparrows will gather beneath the feeders. A suet block will attract woodpeckers, chickadees, nuthatches and, unfortunately, starlings. Often overlooked is the importance of clean, open water for drinking and bathing; this is especially effective in attracting birds during the winter months when natural streams and ponds freeze over. Hummingbird feeders are a very effective way of drawing ruby-throated hummingbirds to your yard (late April through early October).

   Knowing what birds to look for will add to your enjoyment of backyard birding. In addition, by becoming familiar with the common backyard species, you will be better prepared to identify birds in the field. The following birds can be found in Missouri's residential areas.

PERMANENT RESIDENTS

mourning dove	white-breasted nuthatch	Am. goldfinch
rock dove	Carolina wren	house sparrow
downy woodpecker	red-bellied woodpecker	n. mockingbird
northern flicker	eastern screech owl	song sparrow
tufted titmouse	great horned owl	blue jay
American robin	chickadee	European starling
northern cardinal	cedar waxwing (erratic)	house finch
common grackle	brown-headed cowbird	rufous-sided towhee

SUMMER RESIDENTS & VISITORS

house wren	common nighthawk	chipping sparrow
purple martin	ruby-throated hummingbird	yellow warbler
gray catbird	great-crested flycatcher	indigo bunting
chimney swift	brown thrasher	northern oriole
barn swallow	blue-gray gnatcatcher	

WINTER RESIDENTS & VISITORS

brown creeper
pine siskin
hairy woodpecker
golden-cr. kinglet

yellow-bellied sapsucker
yellow-rumped warbler
red-breasted nuthatch
white-throated sparrow

purple finch
dark-eyed junco
evening grosbeak

MIGRANTS
(see Forest and Woodland migrants for specific species)

Swainson's thrush
migrant flycatchers

ruby-crowned kinglet
migrant warblers

white-cr. sparrow
migrant vireos

Northern Flicker, a common resident
of suburban areas
(Photo by Sherm Spoelstra)

III. A GUIDE TO SEASONAL HIGHLIGHTS

Knowing where to go and when to go there is the key to productive bird-watching. This Chapter provides that information by guiding the reader through Missouri's year, directing him/her to the seasonal birding hotspots. This will insure exposure to a large number and variety of birds while also introducing the birder to the State's diverse natural habitats.

Beginning birdwatchers should read through each section before heading into the field. This will let them know what birds they might expect to see and will give them a chance to study identification features for each species. Keep in mind that most of the areas included in this guide are best visited during the morning or late daylight hours; this is especially true during the summer months when birds, like humans, retreat from the mid-day sun.

The following is an outline of the field trips included in this Chapter:

The Vanguard of Spring
> Locations: Grand Pass Conservation Area, Swan Lake National Wildlife Refuge and Fountain Grove Conservation Area
> Time of Year: March
> Highlights: waterfowl migration

Spring in the Bootheel
> Locations: Big Oak Tree State Park, Otter Slough Conservation Area and Mingo National Wildlife Refuge
> Time of Year: April-May
> Highlights: migrant ducks and warblers, wetland birds, ospreys

The Avian Highway
> Locations: Clarence Cannon National Wildlife Refuge and the Ted Shanks Conservation Area
> Time of Year: May-June
> Highlights: migrant warblers and water birds, ospreys

Osage Prairielands
> Locations: Prairie State Park, Schell-Osage C.A. and Taberville Prairie C.A.
> Time of Year: June
> Highlights: upland sandpipers, greater praire chickens, scissor-tailed flycatchers, grassland sparrows

Southern Immigrants
> Location: Ruth & Paul Henning Conservation Area
> Time of Year: July-August
> Highlights: roadrunners, painted buntings

Summer Migration
>Location: Eagle Bluffs Conservation Area
>Time of Year: August-September
>Highlights: shorebird migration, American white pelicans,
>waders, early waterfowl, migrant songbirds

Autumn Woods
>Location: Lake of the Ozarks State Park
>Time of Year: October
>Highlights: woodpeckers, owls, woodland songbirds

Journey to the Sun
>Location: Little Bean Marsh, Smithville Lake and Cooley Lake
>Time of Year: October-November
>Highlights: migrant loons, grebes and waterfowl

A Blizzard of Snows
>Location: Squaw Creek National Wildlife Refuge
>Time of Year: November-December
>Highlights: spectacular flocks of snow geese, other geese and
>ducks, bald eagles, swans

Visitors from the North
>Location: Riverlands Environmental Demonstration Area
>Time of Year: December-January
>Highlights: wintering gulls and ducks, bald eagles,

Winter in the Country
>Location: Charles W. Green Conservation Area, Bradford Farm and
>Little Dixie Lake Conservation Area
>Time of Year: January
>Highlights: falcons, short-eared owls, northern harriers, longspurs,
>possible snow buntings, winter hawks and winter songbirds

The Great Lakes of Missouri
>Locations: Stockton Lake, Pomme de Terre Lake and Truman
>Reservoir
>Time of Year: February
>Highlights: loons, diving ducks, bald eagles

BIRDING AREA LOCATIONS

1. Grand Pass Conservation Area
2. Swan Lake National Wildlife Refuge
3. Fountain Grove Conservation Area
4. Big Oak Tree State Park
5. Otter Slough Conservation Area
6. Mingo National Wildlife Refuge
7. Clarence Cannon National Wildlife Refuge
8. Ted Shanks Conservation Area
9. Prairie State Park
10. Schell-Osage Conservation Area
11. Taberville Prairie Conservation Area
12. Ruth & Paul Henning Conservation Area
13. Eagle Bluffs Conservation Area
14. Lake of the Ozarks State Park
15. Little Bean Marsh Natural History Area
16. Smithville Lake
17. Cooley Lake Conservation Area
18. Squaw Creek National Wildlife Refuge
19. Riverlands Environmental Demonstration Area
20. Charles W. Green Conservation Area
21. Bradford Farm
22. Little Dixie Lake Conservation Area
23. Truman Lake
24. Pomme de Terre Lake
25. Stockton Lake

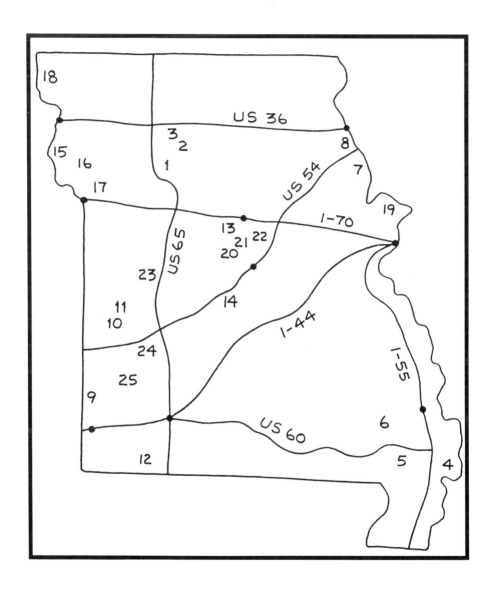

THE VANGUARD OF SPRING
MARCH

March is a fickle month in the American Midwest. As the southern jet stream inches northward, Pacific storms are directed across the Southern Plains; ahead of these storm fronts, warm and moist air from the Gulf of Mexico is swept northward while, in their wake, Canadian air plunges into the Heartland. This scenario produces a constant flux in Missouri's weather, with a mix of raw, windy days, balmy interludes, heavy rains and wet snowfalls.

Since the cold earth cannot absorb this abundant moisture, widespread flooding is common and shallow wetlands spread along the rivers and creeks.   Riding southerly winds ahead of the fronts, huge flocks of waterfowl are drawn to these seasonal wetlands which provide safe and nutritious reststops on their journey to the north. While the migrations of cranes and geese begin in February, the mixed flocks of geese, ducks, coot and grebes peak in March. This is an excellent time to visit three of Missouri's best wetland areas: **Grand Pass Conservation Area**, **Swan Lake National Wildlife Refuge** and **Fountain Grove Conservation Area**.

Directions: From I-70, take Exit 78 and head north on U.S. 65 to Marshall. Pass the city, continuing to the northwest on U.S. 65 for another 7 miles; turn right (north) on Route N and proceed another 5 miles to the Grand Pass Conservation Area (see overview map on the next page).

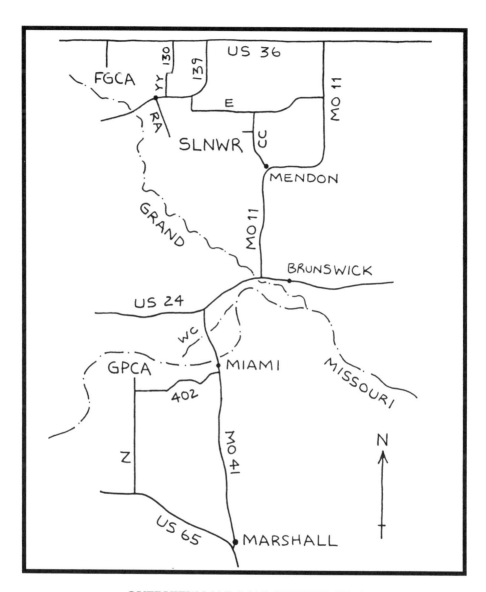

OVERVIEW MAP: MARCH FIELD TRIP

GPCA - GRAND PASS CONSERVATION AREA
SLNWR - SWAN LAKE NAT. WILDLIFE REFUGE
FGCA - FOUNTAIN GROVE CONSERVATION AREA

GRAND PASS CONSERVATION AREA

Covering almost 5300 acres of the Missouri River floodplain, this State Conservation Area is a mosaic of natural and man-made wetlands. A network of earthen dikes and pumps has created a landscape of wet meadows, sloughs and shallow ponds. Crop fields and stands of bottomland forest add to the diversity of this appealing refuge.

The preserve is accessed by dirt/gravel roadways which, in March, can be a bit sloppy and treacherous; a four-wheel drive vehicle will certainly be appreciated on this field trip. Upon entering the Area via Route N, pass the Headquarters Building (HQ) and continue straight ahead (see map on page 29). Large flocks of snow geese are often seen on the wet fields, joined by lesser numbers of Canada and greater white-fronted geese. Mallards, pintail, blue-winged teal and American wigeon area also attracted to these wet meadows. Deeper pools and sloughs attract small flocks of bufflehead, northern shovelers, American coot and lesser scaup.

Watch for killdeer and horned larks along the roadways; the latter are occasionally joined by Lapland longspurs. Northern harriers and red-tailed hawks patrol the open grasslands and bald eagles may be spotted here from November through March. Nearing the Missouri River, the roadway passes through a stand of floodplain woodlands, the domain of red-headed woodpeckers, barred owls, belted kingfishers, American tree sparrows and, by late in March, eastern phoebes.

After completing the 7.5 mile loop, you will arrive back at the Headquarters Building (HQ). Continue straight ahead (eastward) through the intersection and explore the eastern side of the Conservation Area. Once ready to leave, turn east on County Road 402 (see map); this road is not currently marked.

Directions: Follow County Road 402 as it zigzags to the northeast (stay on the main roadway at the various intersections); this road eventually intersects Missouri 41, two miles south of Miami. Turn north (left) on Missouri 41, pass through Miami and cross the Missouri River. On your short drive to U.S. 24, Route 41 crosses the **Wakenda Chute**; stop along the roadway to survey these wetlands for more flocks of waterfowl.

Upon reaching U.S. 24, turn right (east) and drive 7 miles to Missouri 11, on the west side of Brunswick. Turn left (north) on Route 11 and proceed another 10 miles to Mendon. Turn left into Mendon and follow Route CC to the east entrance of **Swan Lake National Wildlife Refuge** (approximately 1.8 miles north of town).

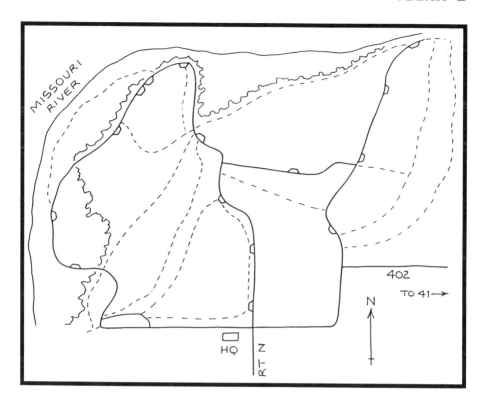

*Gravel roads overlook the sloughs and meadows
of the Grand Pass refuge*

SWAN LAKE NATIONAL WILDLIFE REFUGE

One of more than 500 National Wildlife Refuges, Swan Lake was established in 1937 to protect habitat for migratory and wintering waterfowl. It has since become the primary wintering site for the Eastern Prairie Population of Canada geese which breed in northern Manitoba; more than 100,000 Canada geese winter at the refuge, joined by an excellent variety of other waterfowl species.

Entering the refuge from Route CC, the gravel road soon runs along the southern edge of Silver Lake and its bordering wetlands. Bald eagles often rest in trees along the lake while ring-billed gulls, mergansers, cormorants and diving ducks feed on the open waters. South of the roadway, flooded woodlands attract wood ducks and hooded mergansers; check the trees themselves for red-headed woodpeckers, northern flickers, yellow-rumped warblers and eastern phoebes. Beaver and muskrat dens are common in the shallows of Silver Lake.

In March, the roadway is often flooded at the southwest corner of Silver Lake; if so, backtrack to Route CC and turn left (north). Proceed to Route E and turn left (west). You will soon cross the floodplain of Elk Creek which, by mid-March, is usually an elongated lake. Flocks of shallow-water ducks (mallards, pintails, wigeon, shovelers) are often found here.

Continue westward on E and then continue west on Road 114 to either of the northern entrances (see map on the next page). The interior of the refuge is closed to visitors from October 15 to January 15; by March, you can follow the roadways to the west shore of Silver Lake, across the central cropfields and around the basin of Swan Lake. Watch for killdeer, horned larks and eastern meadowlarks along these roads and scan the fields for flocks of snow geese, Canada geese and ducks. Northern harriers, red-tailed hawk, rough-legged hawks and an occasional short-eared owl hunt on these fields; rare visitors such as snowy owls might be found early in the month.

The roadway crosses the Elk Creek drainage southeast of Swan Lake; these shallows attract a variety of ducks (mallards, teal, hooded mergansers, buffleheads), American coot and pied-billed grebes. Coot are also common along the west edge of Swan Lake. Mixed flocks of redheads, canvasbacks, ring-necked ducks and lesser scaup gather on deeper waters of the refuge or may appear in flooded areas west of Swan Lake.

The refuge Visitor Center (VC) is open on weekdays, from 8am-4:30pm, and an observation tower, just east of the Center, offers a panorama of Swan Lake and its adjacent wetlands.

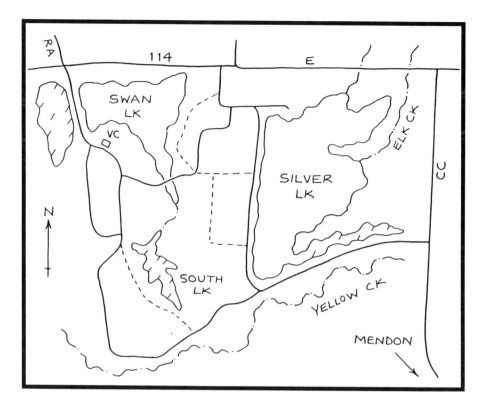

A snowy March at Swan Lake

Directions: From the northwest corner of the National Wildlife Refuge, head north on Route RA and drive into Sumner. Turn right on Missouri 139 N and proceed almost 2 miles to YY. Turn left (north) on YY (which becomes Missouri 130) and drive 9.5 miles to U.S. 36; the last few miles of this route pass through Pershing State Park.

Turn left (west) on U.S. 36 and drive 5 miles to Route W. Turn left (south) on Route W and drive 3.5 miles to the junction with Belt Rd.; you can then proceed to areas of interest in Fountain Grove Conservation Area, as illustrated on its map.

FOUNTAIN GROVE CONSERVATION AREA

Located at the junction of Locust Creek and the Grand River, this 7154 acre refuge is a composite of floodplain wetlands, controlled marshlands, lakes and ponds, accessed by a network of gravel roads and levees. Extensive flooding in March closes access to some portions of the preserve but birding can be excellent around Che-Ru Lake and at the office complex (see map).

Proceed east on Belt Road to Crown Road and turn right (south). Pass the intersection with Bunker Road and continue south to Che-Ru Lake. Views of the lake are obtained from the boat-ramp access road or, better yet, from a one-way levee road that runs along the southern and eastern sides of the lake (see map). Bald eagles still fish on the lake in March and double-crested cormorants are usually found here by the middle of the month. Small flocks of diving ducks (lesser scaup, buffleheads, ring-necked ducks and hooded mergansers) often rest and feed on the lake. The levee road also provides an overview of wetlands east of Che-Ru Lake; scan these wooded swamps and marshes for mallards, pintail, northern shovelers, American coot, American widgeon, green-winged and blue-winged teal, common snipe and gadwall. Drowned trees in the area attract a variety of woodpeckers and the wooded swamps offer prime habitat for eastern phoebes, American tree sparrows, winter wrens, yellow-rumped warblers and rusty blackbirds.

After circling Che-Ru Lake, drive west on Bunker Road to Route W and Blackhorn Drive (see map). Turn left and proceed to the Headquarters complex which sits above the Grand River floodplain. In March, the River usually spills across this valley, creating extensive shallows and attracting huge rafts of waterfowl. Ring-necked ducks, redheads and lesser scaup are often abundant here, joined by a wide variety of other waterfowl. Lucky birders may spot a peregrine falcon as it streaks across the marsh, hoping to snare an unwary victim.

*Che-Ru Lake attracts bald eagles, cormorants
and migrant waterfowl*

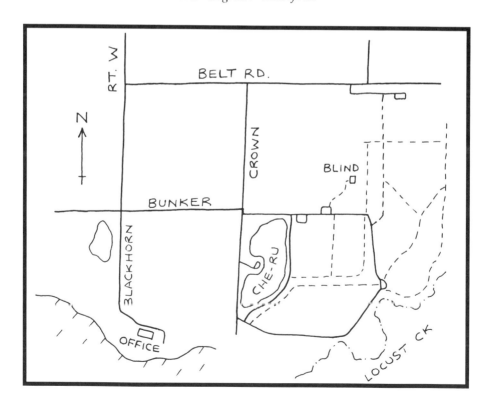

SPRING IN THE BOOTHEEL
APRIL-MAY

Wetlands are this planet's crucibles of life. They provide breeding grounds for most of earth's insects, terrestrial invertebrates and amphibians and are home to a wide variety of reptiles, birds and mammals. Nevertheless, swamps and marshlands are continually threatened by the activities of modern man; drainage, development, stream diversion and pollution all take a toll.

Missouri harbors an excellent diversity of natural and restored wetlands which are important staging areas for migrant waterfowl and shorebirds. April through early May is a good time to visit these areas as the tide of spring sweeps northward and a new cycle of life begins. The migrant waterfowl are joined by the first wave of summer songbirds while, in adjacent woodlands, owls and eagles are already busy with their ravenous young. Hibernating mammals are reappearing on the wet meadows and the warming earth draws amphibians and reptiles from their winter retreats.

I suggest a field trip to three refuges in southeast Missouri: **Big Oak Tree State Park**, **Otter Slough Conservation Area** and **Mingo National Wildlife Refuge**.

Directions: From I-55, 8 miles south of Sikeston, take Exit 58 and head east on Missouri 80. Drive 11.7 miles, passing through East Prairie, and turn right (south) on Missouri 102. Proceed another 11.3 miles and turn right on Route RB; this road leads into Big Oak Tree State Park (see map).

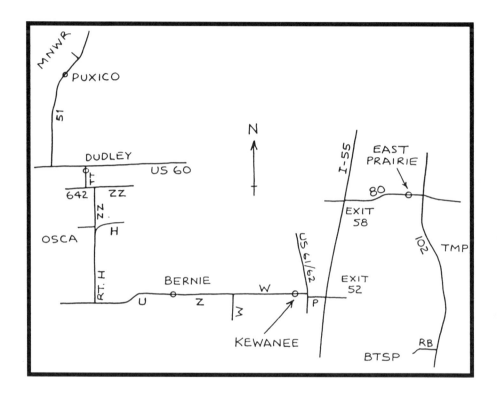

OVERVIEW MAP: APRIL-MAY FIELD TRIP

BTSP - BIG OAK TREE STATE PARK
OSCA - OTTER SLOUGH CONSERVATION AREA
MNWR - MINGO NAT. WILDLIFE REFUGE

BIG OAK TREE STATE PARK

When the first white explorers reached the Mississippi Valley, a rich swamp forest covered much of the River's floodplain, interspersed with pockets of open marsh and wet meadow. The moist, nutritious soil supported the growth of huge trees, dominated by water-loving species such as burr oak, silver maple, American sycamore and bald cypress.

Timber production, agriculture and swamp drainage destroyed most of these floodplain woodlands by the early 1930s, prompting a group of southeast Missouri residents to fund the protection of a 1007-acre stand of virgin swamp forest in Mississippi County. Now contained within Big Oak Tree State Park, this fabulous woodland contains twelve Missouri State Champion Trees, two of which are also National Champions. A fine boardwalk leads visitors among these towering giants and provides an excellent avenue for birding.

Pileated woodpeckers, wild turkey, barred owls, Carolina wrens, eastern screech owls and red-headed woodpeckers are among the Park's permanent residents. During the warmer months, they are joined by hooded warblers, red-eyed vireos, Kentucky warblers, Mississippi kites, prothonotary warblers, Louisiana waterthrushes and common yellowthroats. Swainson's warblers nest here, attracted to stands of giant cane that dot the understory.

After completing the boardwalk, stop by the Park's lake, which is studded with baldcypress trees. Ospreys, double-crested cormorants and hooded mergansers often fish here. Fish crows may also be found in this area.

Directions: From Big Oak Tree State Park, return to Missouri 102 and head north. If time permits, you may want to stop at **Ten Mile Pond Conservation Area**, which stretches east from Route 102, 5 miles south of Missouri 80. Seasonal wetlands, accessed by a network of levees, attract a variety of migrant waterfowl to this area.

Return to Missouri 80, turn left (west) and proceed back to I-55. Turn south on the Interstate and drive to Exit 52. Head west toward Kewanee; after driving .7 mile, turn right and then take an immediate left onto Route W, continuing toward Kewanee. Proceed through town and continue westward for 8 miles to the junction with Route Z. Continue westward on Route Z to the town of Bernie (14 miles); change to Route U, continuing to the west for another 6.7 miles. Turn right (north) on Route H and drive 4.4 miles to Route ZZ. Change to Route ZZ and take an immediate left on the entry road to **Otter Slough Conservation Area**.

*The boardwalk at
Big Oak Tree
State Park*

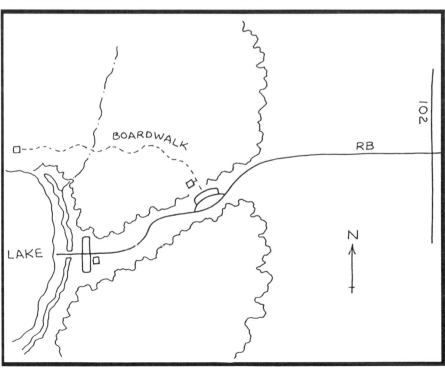

OTTER SLOUGH CONSERVATION AREA

Covering 4866 acres of the St. Francis River valley, Otter Slough Conservation Area was established to stem the loss of wetland ecosystems in southeast Missouri and to provide habitat for migratory and wintering waterfowl.   Most of the area stretches southward from Otter Lake, a cypress-
tupelo swamp; visitors will find a mosaic of ponds, sloughs, wet meadows,
marsh, crop fields, canals, seasonal wetlands and stands of bottomland
forest at this refuge.

In April, large flocks of waterfowl still move about the preserve, resting on
open waters or feeding in the marshlands and crop fields. Gadwall, coot,
mallards, shovelers and blue-winged teal are abundant, joined by smaller
flocks of wigeon, pintail and green-winged teal. Cypress Lake, a man-made
impoundment, attracts pied-billed grebes, double-crested cormorants, lesser
scaup and an occasional flock of white pelicans.

A nature trail (NT) leads along the south shore of Otter Lake and loops
through the bottomland forest. Look for migrant ospreys in the baldcypress
trees and scan the open waters for wood ducks and hooded mergansers. The
moist woodland offers choice habitat for barred owls, red-shouldered
hawks, woodpeckers, eastern phoebes, blue-gray gnatcatchers, prothonotary
warblers, Acadian flycatchers and other riparian songbirds; migrant warblers and vireos can be abundant here in early May.

Wet fields and mudflats cover much of the refuge, making it an ideal rest-
stop for migrant shorebirds. Killdeer, spotted sandpipers, pectoral sandpipers, lesser yellowlegs, solitary sandpipers and least sandpipers are
among the more common species; rice fields on the east side of Road 675 may
harbor black-necked stilts or American avocets. Check the marshy shallows for American and least bitterns, herons, soras and an occasional rail.
Eastern meadowlarks, horned larks, red-winged blackbirds, barn swallows
and field sparrows are easily found along the roadways where northern
harriers and red-tailed hawks patrol the grasslands.

Directions: From Otter Slough Conservation Area, return to Route ZZ and
head north. Drive 2 miles and turn left (west) on Road 642. Proceed 1 mile
and turn right (north) on TT. Drive 3 miles to Dudley and head west on U.S.
60. Proceed 5.3 miles and exit onto Missouri 51. Head north on 51; the entrance to **Mingo National Wildlife Refuge** will be 13.7 miles ahead, on your
left.

*Open wetlands
at Otter Slough*

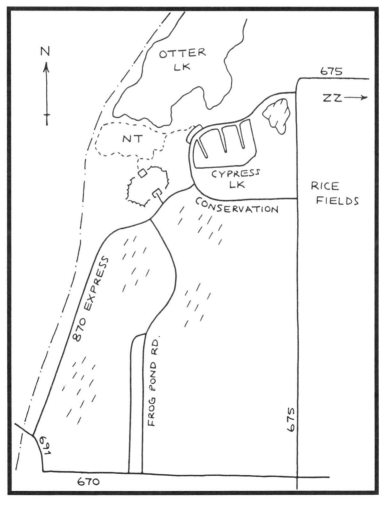

MINGO NATIONAL WILDLIFE REFUGE

Sprawling across the former channel of the Mississippi River, this 21,676 acre preserve was established to protect vital wetland habitat and to offer refuge for migrant and wintering waterfowl. Today, it is well known to naturalists for its excellent variety of birdlife as well as for the many reptiles, amphibians and mammals that inhabit its swamps, marshes and woodlands. Man-made levees and canals are used to control water flow through the refuge, yielding ideal conditions for the production of crops, mast and natural grains.

Bald eagles, trumpeter swans, tundra swans and snow geese are among the winter visitors at Mingo while year-round residents include river otters, bobcat, mink, beaver, wild turkey, barred owls, wood ducks and hooded mergansers. The refuge is one of the better areas in Missouri to find barn owls and has been known to attract rare summer visitors such as anhingas, roseate spoonbills and fulvous whistling ducks.

Spring is an excellent time to visit Mingo National Wildlife Refuge. Migrants are passing through, summer residents have arrived and the permanent residents are especially active. Be sure to stop by the **Nature Center (NC)** for an introduction to the refuge and plan to take the 20-mile Auto Tour which leads past the varied habitats of the fabulous preserve; a day use fee of $3.00 per vehicle is charged. The **Auto Tour (AT)** route is open from 8am to 4pm, April, May, October and November.

Descend from the Nature Center and head southwest on Bluff Road (see map). Stop at the **Boardwalk Nature Trail (BWT)** for a 1 mile excursion through bottomland forest and out to the edge of **Rockhouse Marsh (RM)**. Barred owls, pileated woodpeckers, eastern phoebes, brown thrashers, gray catbirds, prothonotary warblers, cuckoos and blue-gray gnatcatchers are among the forest residents. Be sure to take the side trail that leads out to an overlook of the marsh; belted kingfishers, eastern kingbirds, Mississippi kites, soras, common moorhens, least bitterns, herons and egrets may be viewed from the deck and mink often hunt in this area.

Continue southwestward on Bluff Road where a series of **overlooks (V)** provide changing views of Rockhouse Marsh. You will soon reach a meadow area where the road begins a 1-way loop (see map); cattle graze in this area and may be accompanied by cattle egrets. Continue along the Auto Tour as it angles to the west, crosses the Mingo River and then fords a spillway. The narrow road now begins a steady climb onto a wooded ridge that rises along the west edge of the refuge; several **overlooks (V)** offer expansive views of Monopoly Lake, Rockhouse Marsh and the Mingo Valley, all backed by the low hills of Crowley's Ridge.

Just past May Pond, the Auto Tour angles to the east, descending past **Monopoly Lake**. Bald eagles now nest along the lake and ospreys fish on the open waters in spring and fall. Moist woodlands along section of the Mingo River valley attract an excellent variety of migrant songbirds in late April and early May. Complete the 1-way loop and turn left on Bluff Road.

Rockhouse Marsh

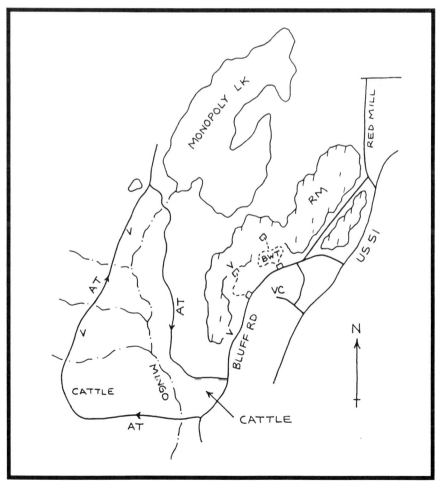

THE AVIAN HIGHWAY
MAY-JUNE

Flowing north to south through the heart of our Continent, the Mississippi River has long been a natural corridor for bird migration. More than a flight path, the River's floodplain, with its swamp forests, wet meadows, oxbow lakes and shallow marshlands, provides an attrative mix of reststops for avian travellers. Woodlands attract migrant warblers, flycatchers, orioles and other songbirds while the ponds, lakes and marshes are natural magnets for herons, egrets, rails, terns, cormorants, pelicans, shorebirds and water-fowl.

Two refuges in northeast Missouri, the **Clarence Cannon National Wildlife Refuge** and the **Ted Shanks Conservation Area**, are excellent destinations to observe spring migrants along the Mississippi. While I recommend a visit in early to mid May, flooding can limit access in some years and you may need to postpone your visit until early June; call ahead to check on conditions:

Clarence Cannon National Wildlife Refuge: 573-847-2333
Ted Shanks Conservation Area: 573-754-6171

Seasonal wetlands along the Mississippi River
are vital to migrant birds

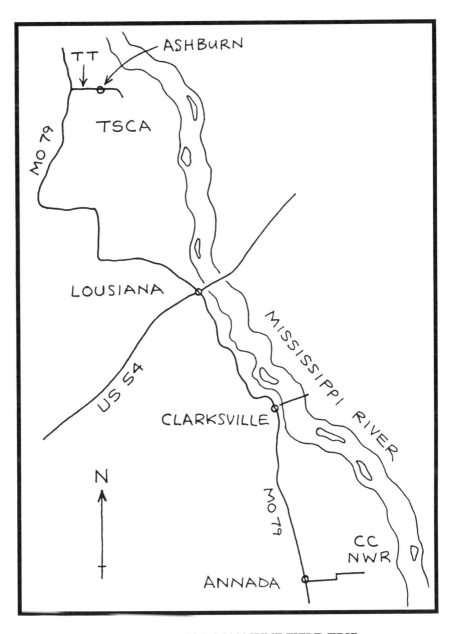

OVERVIEW MAP: MAY-JUNE FIELD TRIP

TSCA - TED SHANKS CONSERVATION AREA
CCNWR - CLARENCE CANNON N.W.R.

CLARENCE CANNON NATIONAL WILDLIFE REFUGE

Established in 1964 to protect habitat for nesting wood ducks and migrant waterfowl, Clarence Cannon National Wildlife Refuge covers 3752 acres of the Mississippi River floodplain. Its mosaic of wetland habitats attracts over 200 species of birds in the course of a year and provides refuge for muskrat, beaver, mink, coyotes, opossum and raccoons. In recent years, a pair of bald eagles has nested at the preserve.

May is an excellent time to visit Clarence Cannon. Summer residents have arrived and spring migrants, including late waterfowl, shorebirds, terns and warblers stop to rest and feed at the refuge.

Directions: The entry road to Clarence Cannon National Wildlife Refuge leads east from Annada, which sits on Missouri 79, nine miles south of Clarksville. Within 1/2 mile, the graveled road jogs to the north and then continues eastward for another mile to the Refuge Headquarters (HQ). The preserve, itself is accessed by a network of gravel roads and field trails (see map).

Summer residents at Clarence Cannon include least bitterns, black-crowned and yellow-crowned night herons, great egrets, king rails, soras, American woodcocks, yellow-billed cuckoos, purple martins, all regional swallows, Acadian flycatchers, eastern kingbirds, eastern phoebes, American redstarts, northern and orchard orioles, prothonotary warblers and common yellowthroats. Among the permanent residents are wood ducks, hooded mergansers, wild turkeys, bald eagles, great blue herons, red-shouldered hawks, barred owls, eastern screech owls, red-headed woodpeckers and loggerhead shrikes.

Spring migrants of note include ospreys, peregrine falcons, American white pelicans, double-crested cormorants, migrant shorebirds, black terns, white-crowned sparrows and a superb variety of warblers. Snowy egrets, little blue herons, American bitterns and cattle egrets often visit the refuge during the warmer months of the year.

Directions: After exploring Clarence Cannon National Wildlife Refuge, return to Missouri 79 and head north. Pass through Clarksville and continue to Louisiana. Continue north for another 14 miles and turn right onto Route TT. Proceed 1 mile into Ashburn and continue straight ahead to the entrance for the **Ted Shanks Conservation Area.**

*Shallow sloughs are magnets for shorebirds,
herons, egrets and waterfowl*

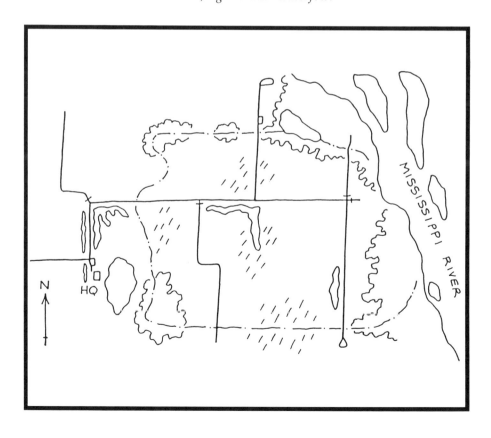

TED SHANKS CONSERVATION AREA

Acquired in the early 1970s, this 6705 acre refuge is managed by the Missouri Department of Conservation, in cooperation with the U.S. Fish & Wildlife Service and the U.S. Army Corps of Engineers. Composed of natural and man-made wetlands, this fabulous preserve is located at the confluence of the Salt and Mississippi Rivers, in Pike County.

Its varied habitat, from open marsh to floodplain woodlands, is laced by 35 miles of levees and 9 miles of canals. An 11.5 mile **Auto Tour Road (AT)**, loops through the refuge, taking the visitor past its component habitats and ensuring exposure to a superb variety of wildlife.

River otters, beaver and muskrat are among the resident mammals. Nesting birds of note include least and Amerian bitterns, king rails, pied-billed grebes, American coot, wood ducks, little blue herons, hooded mergansers, Cooper's hawks, red-shouldered hawks, American woodcock, ruffed grouse, wild turkey, whip-poor-wills, willow flycatchers, Bell's vireos, ovenbirds, worm-eating warblers, bobolinks, blue grosbeaks, lark sparrows and Le-Conte's sparrows; bald eagles have nested here since 1997.

Among the many spring migrants at Ted Shanks are horned and eared grebes, American white pelicans, white-faced ibis, cattle egrets, sora, Virginia rails, migrant shorebirds, ospreys, Bonaparte's gulls, Caspian and black terns, gray-cheeked thrushes, solitary vireos, migrant warblers, Brewer's blackbirds and sharp-tailed sparrows.

Common residents, such as great-blue herons, green-backed herons, great egrets, barn and tree swallows, eastern bluebirds, eastern meadowlarks, belted kingfishers, wood thrushes, house wrens, rose-breasted grosbeaks, indigo buntings, warbling vireos and grasshopper sparrows, round-out the bird population. Plan to stop by the **Headquarters Building (HQ)** for an overview of the preserve's vital role in habitat protection and wildlife conservation.

A spring storm gathers above the wetlands

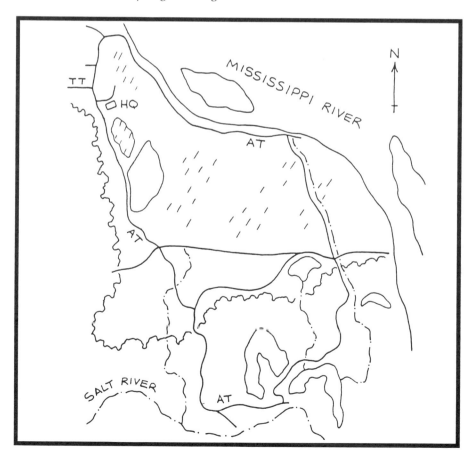

OSAGE PRAIRIELANDS
JUNE

As the last of the Pleistocene Glaciers, the Wisconsin, retreated into Canada, 10,000 years ago, a vast grassland stretched from western Ohio to the foot of the Rocky Mountains. Nourished by glacial till and maintained by periodic wildfires, a rich, tallgrass prairie flourished across the Upper Midwest, including northern and western Missouri. At the peak of its development, more than 13 million acres of tallgrass prairie covered parts of our State; today, most has succumbed to the farmer's plow and only 65,000 acres remain.

The largest and best prairie remnants are found across the Osage Plain of western Missouri. Unglaciated, the thin, rocky soils of this region were less attractive for crop production and most of the Osage grasslands were used for ranching. As a result, the native prairie was less impacted and devoted conservationists have since worked to protect some of the better areas.

June is a good time to visit the Osage prairielands. Grassland birds and mammals are especially active, attending to their young, and prairie wildflowers adorn the landscape. Among the latter are coneflowers, rattlesnake master, Indian paintbrush, white prairie clover, beard-tongue and shooting star. Prairie mammals include coyote, bobcat, white-tailed deer, red fox, badger, skunk, prairie voles, harvest mice, cottontail rabbits and little brown bats. Among the grassland reptiles are ornate box turtles, fence and glass lizards, six-lined racerunners, prairie king snakes, yellow-bellied racers and prairie ringneck snakes.

For an overview of the prairie birdlife, I suggest visiting three preserves across the Osage Plain: **Prairie State Park**, the **Schell-Osage Conservation Area** and the **Taberville Prairie Conservation Area**.

Directions: From U.S. 71, at Lamar, exit onto U.S. 160 and head west. Drive 12 miles, watching for scissor-tailed flycatchers and upland sandpipers on the fences and wires. Turn right (north) on Route NN, proceed 1 mile and turn left (west) on Central Road; this road runs along and near the southern border of **Prairie State Park** (see map on page 51).

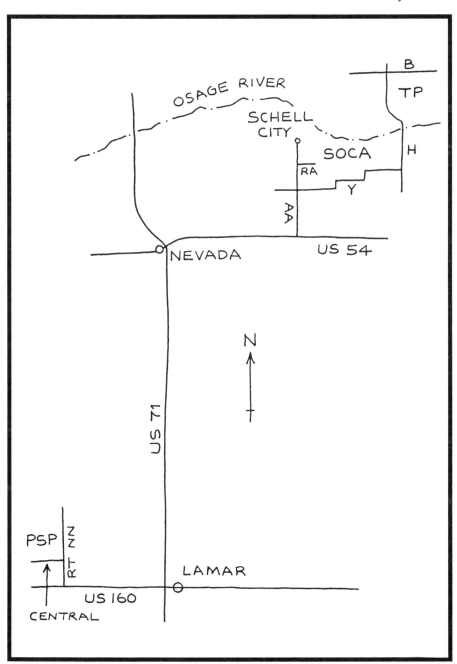

OVERVIEW MAP: JUNE FIELD TRIP

PSP - PRAIRIE STATE PARK
SOCA - SCHELL-OSAGE CONSERVATION AREA
TP - TABERVILLE PRAIRIE CONSERVATION AREA

PRAIRIE STATE PARK

Harboring the largest prairie remnant in Missouri, Prairie State Park is more remniscent of a National Wildlife Refuge. This remote preserve, which covers more than 3700 acres, is characterized by open grasslands, laced with streamside shrub communities and parcels of woodland. Its unique nature is further enhanced by a resident bison herd, introduced in 1982 to maintain the quality of this prairie ecosystem.

More than 350 species of grasses and wildflowers can be found across the prairie which is home to coyotes, red fox, badgers, ornate box turtles, bullsnakes, six-lined racerunners, southern plains skinks, prairie crayfish and prairie voles. Access to the vast preserve is provided by a fine network of trails (see map); check at the **Visitor Center (VC)** before your hike, since trails are closed in areas where the bison are grazing. Non-hikers will find many of the Park's birds along Central Road (see map), where some perch on the wires and others feed among the shrubs.

More than 150 bird species have been identified at Prairie State Park. Among the permanent residents are northern harriers, red-tailed hawks, American kestrels, greater prairie chickens, northern bobwhites, great horned owls, horned larks, loggerhead shrikes, rufous-sided towhees, eastern bluebirds, eastern meadowlarks and field sparrows. Joining them during the warmer months are yellow-billed cuckoos, whip-poor-wills, chuck-wills-widows, upland sandpipers, eastern and western kingbirds, scissor-tailed flycatchers, least flycatchers, Bell's vireos, yellow-breasted chats, blue-winged warblers, indigo buntings, blue grosbeaks, Henslow's sparrows, grasshopper sparrows, orchard orioles and dickcissels. Swainson's hawks and Mississippi kites may also visit the refuge. The Park's greater prairie chickens are perhaps best found in the **East Drywood Natural Area** (see map).

Directions: From Prairie State Park, drive back to U.S. 71 and head north to Nevada. Exit onto U.S. 54 East and proceed 11.7 miles to Route AA (at Dederick) and turn left (north). Drive 11 miles on AA, crossing open country where a number of species, including scissor-tailed flycatchers, will be found on the roadside wires. Turn right (east) on Route RA and proceed into the **Schell-Osage Conservation Area.**

Prairie State Park: Big Sky country

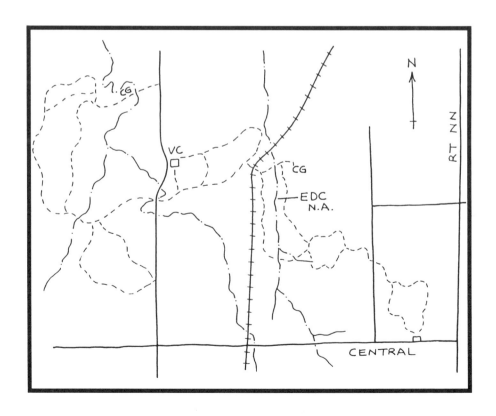

SCHELL-OSAGE CONSERVATION AREA

Opened to the public in 1964, this diverse 8600 acre preserve stretches along the Osage River. Half of the refuge is covered by bottomland woods and swampland while the southern half is a mix of upland forest, meadows, ponds, lakes and prairie remnants.

While Schell and Atkinson Lakes attract ospreys and waterfowl during the spring and fall migrations, June occupants include great blue herons, green-backed herons, mallards and wood ducks. A resident population of 1500 Canada geese also use these lakes.

North and east of Schell Lake, a chain of wooded swamps, wet meadows and open marshlands line the roadways. This is a good area to find killdeer, spotted sandpipers, eastern kingbirds, yellow-billed cuckoos, belted kingfishers, common yellowthroats and a variety of flycatchers. Drowned woodlands attract red-headed woodpeckers and provide nest sites for tree swallows, eastern bluebirds and prothonotary warblers. Lewis' woodpeckers, rare visitors to Missouri, have been spotted at the refuge in recent years.

South of Atkinson Lake, upland woods, meadows and prairie remnants pre-dominate. Northern bobwhites, horned larks, American kestrels, eastern bluebirds, scissor-tailed flycatchers, eastern meadowlarks, indigo buntings, brown thrashers and field sparrows are often spotted along the roads and trails. Turkey vultures, northern harriers and red-tailed hawks patrol the open areas, replaced by great horned owls as dusk envelops the refuge.

Directions: Pick up Route Y at the southeast edge of the Schell-Osage Con-servation Area (see map) and head east to Route H. Turn left (north) on Route H and proceed 4.6 miles to the west access lot for the **Taberville Prairie Conservation Area**.

Flooded timber along the Osage River

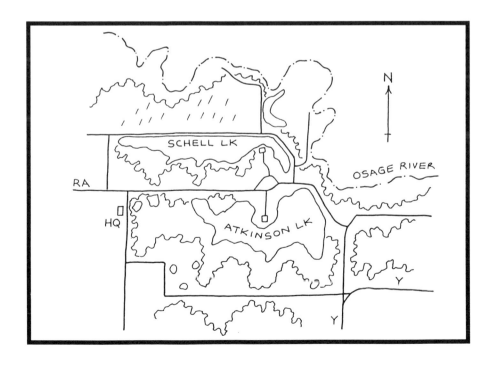

TABERVILLE PRAIRIE CONSERVATION AREA

Purchased by the Missouri Department of Conservation in 1959, Taberville Prairie was the first prairie remnant obtained to protect habitat for greater prairie chickens. Covering 1680 acres, this native grassland has been designated both a Missouri Natural Area and a National Natural Landmark.

More than 400 native plants characterize the preserve, which is characterized by tallgrass prairie and streamside shrub communities. The spring fed streams are home to the rare blacknose shiner and four State endangered plants can be found at the refuge: pale-green orchids, yellow-eyed grass, Mead's milkweed and geocarpon.

Foot-trails lead into the preserve from parking lots on Route H and on County Road NW 1001 (see map). In addition to the greater prairie chickens, look for northern harriers, red-tailed hawks, northern bobwhites, eastern bluebirds, loggerhead shrikes, scissor-tailed flycatchers, eastern meadowlarks, field sparrows, Henslow's sparrows, dickcissels and savannah sparrows in the open areas. Check the streamside shrub communities for eastern kingbirds, American goldfinches, indigo buntings, yellow-breasted chats, Bell's vireos, yellow warblers, song sparrows and common yellowthroats.

Directions: After exploring the Taberville Prairie, the State's major highway system is best reached by heading east on Route B (see map); Missouri 13, at Osceola, will be 16 miles ahead.

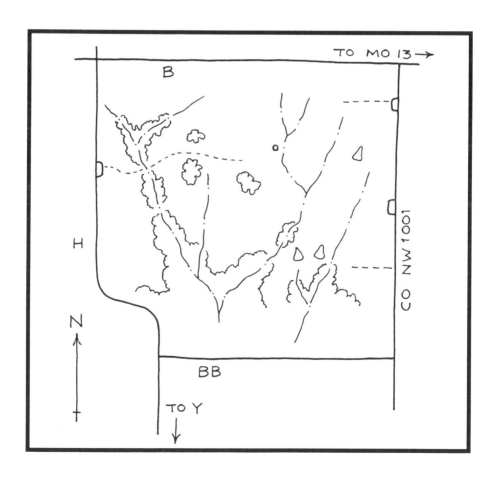

SOUTHERN IMMIGRANTS
JULY-AUGUST

As the North American climate gradually warmed following the Pleisto-cene Epoch, plant and animal species began to move northward, occupying lands that were once locked in ice. Even today, certain birds and mammals are expanding their range, adapting to new habitats.

Among the more well known immigrants are the Virginia opossum and the nine-banded armadillo, both of which have migrated northward from the southern States. Cattle egrets, having reached Florida in the 1950s, con-tinue to expand their range to the north and west. Even the well-known cardinal was once restricted to southern areas of North America.

In Missouri, painted buntings and greater roadrunners are relative new-comers and are still restricted to our southernmost counties; the former is a summer resident while the latter inhabits southwest Missouri throughout the year. Ironically, one of the best places to find these southern immigrants is amidst one of the State's most developed and congested areas....Branson, Missouri.

RUTH & PAUL HENNING CONSERVATION AREA

Tucked away from the gaudy congestion of Branson is the Ruth & Paul Hen-ning Conservation Area, a 1534 acre refuge managed by the Missouri Depart-ment of Conservation. This scenic preserve drops northeastward from Mis-souri 76 and protects some of the States best limestone glades.

Characterized by thin, rocky soil above sheets of limestone bedrock, these glades are best developed on sunny, south-facing slopes. Prairie wildflow-ers, including wild blue indigo, Missouri primrose, prairie dock , coneflowers and Indian paintbrush, adorn the open glades which are under assault by expanding cedar groves. Selective clearing of the cedar is used to maintain a balance between woodland and glade communities. Among the more inter-esting flora at Henning are American smoketrees, some of which live up to 300 years.

The refuge is accessed by three trail loops, two of which begin at the over-look area off Missouri 76 (see map). A paved, 1/2 mile trail loops to a tower atop Dewey Bald while the 1.6 mile **Glade Trail (GT)** runs through the varied habitats of the refuge; a connector trail shortens the loop to 1 mile.

American crows, northern flickers, eastern kingbirds, wild turkey, greater roadrunners, cedar waxwings, painted buntings, indigo buntings, yellow-breasted chats, eastern bluebirds and rufous-sided towhees characterize the bird population. Other residents include eastern collared lizards, taran-tulas and scorpions.

Directions: From U.S. 65 at Branson, exit onto Missouri 76 and head west, driving through the heart of this entertainment mecca; the Henning Conser-vation Area will be almost 4 miles ahead, on your right, accessed by the Scenic Overlook drive. Plan an early morning visit to avoid local traffic.

Limestone glades cloak the hillsides

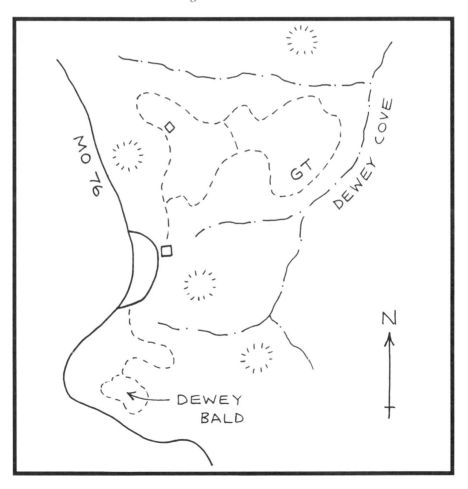

SUMMER MIGRANTS
AUGUST-SEPTEMBER

The fall bird migration actually begins in July, as the first wave of shore-birds depart their Arctic breeding grounds and funnel toward southern coasts. They are soon joined by "freeze-sensitive" songbirds (those that feed on nectar and insects) and by early waterfowl such as blue-winged and cinnamon teal. By late summer, other birds, such as American white pelicans, double-crested cormorants, great egrets, cattle egrets, black terns and Franklin's gulls begin to gather in large flocks, resting and feeding at reservoirs before their long journey to the south. One of the better places to witness these summer maneuvers in at Eagle Bluffs Conservation Area, in central Missouri.

EAGLE BLUFFS CONSERVATION AREA

This refuge is a 4269 acre peninsula of natural and man-controlled wetlands on the Missouri River floodplain. Characterized by shallow channels, sloughs, ponds, marsh, croplands and moist woodlands, the preserve is a magnet for migrant shorebirds and waterfowl. Access is provided by a network of gravel roads, levees and field trails (see map).

Large flocks of great blue herons and great egrets gather at this refuge in late summer. They are joined by lesser numbers of green-backed herons, soras, American bitterns, migrant rails and the occasional snowy egret. Mixed flocks of shorebirds alight on the expanding mudflats while the deeper pools attract cormorants, American white pelicans and terns (black, Forster's, common and Caspian). Turkey vultures, drawn to the area by stranded schools of fish, are abundant here in late summer.

Riparian woodlands along the Missouri River and Perche Creek fill with songbirds and an early morning visit should turn up northern orioles, rose-breasted grosbeaks, ruby-throated hummingbirds, house wrens, eastern wood pewees, warbling vireos, and a variety of migrants. Belted kingfishers, red-headed woodpeckers, barred owls and wood ducks also inhabit the floodplain timber. Out on the fields and croplands, American crows, mourning doves, red-winged blackbirds, American goldfinches, barn swallows, American kestrels and horned larks will be found. Northern harriers and red-tailed hawks are common at Eagle Bluffs and the patient birder may find a merlin or peregrine falcon. Check the Perche Creek bridge area for cliff and bank swallows.

By mid September, large flocks of blue-winged teal arrive at Eagle Bluffs, soon to be followed by the men that hunt them. That's our clue to move on to State Parks and protected areas.

Directions: From I-70 in Columbia, take Exit 126 and head south on Providence Road. Drive 5.5 miles and angle southwestward on Route K. Proceed another 7.5 miles to McBaine. A lot in McBaine services the Katy Trail, which runs along the east side of Eagle Bluffs, paralleling Perche Creek. To enter the Conservation Area, continue westward on Route K to Star School Road (SSR; see map).

*Drowned cottonwoods
rise above a channel
at Eagle Bluffs*

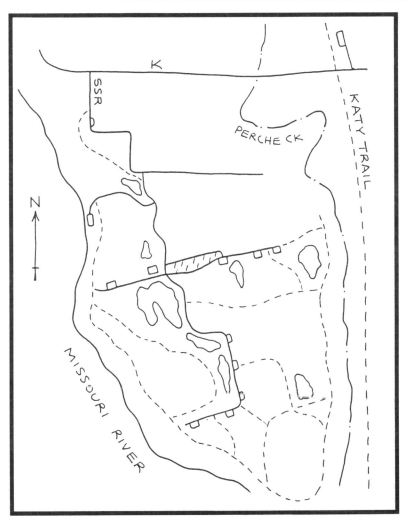

AUTUMN WOODS
OCTOBER

Can there be a naturalist alive who doesn't love the month of October? Its warm, sunny days, colorful foliage and clear, cool nights can entice even the most dedicated couch potato into the great outdoors! Of course, October also heralds the onset of hunting season and I recommend that birders head for State Parks and other protected refuges.

Missouri offers many excellent forest preserves for hikers and naturalists, most of which are concentrated across the Ozark Plateau. I have selected Lake of the Ozarks State Park due to its central location, ease of access and fine trail network.

LAKE OF THE OZARKS STATE PARK

Spaced around the Grand Glaize arm of the Lake of the Ozarks, Missouri's largest State Park covers more than 17,000 acres. A rich, hardwood forest cloaks most of the Park, complemented by springs, caves, bluffs and dolomite glades. An overview map, on the next page, illustrates the location of access roads and parking lots; while many miles of hiking trails lace the Park, I recommend three of them for birders: the **Bluestem Knoll Savanna (BKS)**, the **Squaw's Revenge Trail (SRT)** and the **Rocky Top Trail (RTT)**.

Directions: From U.S. 54 in Osage Beach, head southeast on Missouri 42 and proceed 3.5 miles to Route 134. Turn right (south) on 134 for access to the Bluestem Knoll Savanna and the Squaw's Revenge Trail.

To reach the Rocky Top Trail, continue southwest on U.S. 54 from the Missouri 42 junction. Drive 4.4 miles and turn left on Grand Glaize Beach Road; nearing the beach, bear right and head up to the picnic area where you will find the trailhead for the Rocky Top Trail.

Rich forest and lake views reward your visit

A ridgetop glade along the Rocky Top Trail

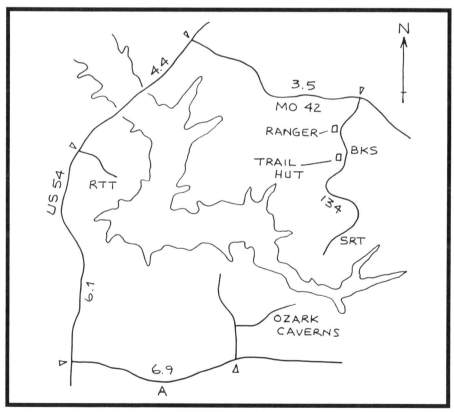

OVERVIEW MAP
LAKE OF THE OZARKS STATE PARK

Bluestem Knoll Savanna - This small, ridgetop savanna, characterized by prairie grasses and wildflowers, is accessed by a .5 mile trail loop. Birders should find a mix of open woodland species in this area, including northern flickers, northern bobwhites, blue jays, Carolina chickadees, northern mockingbirds, northern cardinals, dark-eyed juncos, white-throated sparrows and American goldfinches. It is also a good area to look for transients such as ruby-crowned kinglets, cedar waxwings and white-crowned sparrows.

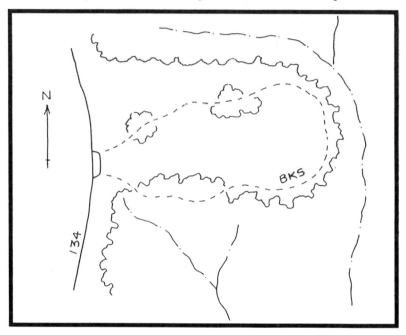

Squaw's Revenge Trail - One of the best trail loops within the Park, this 2-mile route begins and ends at the horse corral, across from the stables. Most of the path leads through mature, deciduous forest, dipping in and out of ravines. Watch for all woodpecker species, tufted titmice, Carolina chickadees, white-breasted nuthatches, brown creepers, golden-crowned kinglets, yellow-rumped warblers and hermit thrushes along the trail. Nearing bluffs along the lake, you are likely to scare turkey vultures from their roosts. Once atop the bluffs, you are treated to broad views of the lake; scan the scene for ospreys that stop to fish here during migrations. Returning to the forest, the path merges with the Trail of Four Winds (TFW) for a short distance; watch for wild turkeys and white-tailed deer in this area. Complete the trail loop and return to your car.

MAP ⟶

Rocky Top Trail - This 3 mile, double-loop trail begins and ends at the Picnic Area just south of Grand Glaize Beach (see map). The path climbs westward from the parking area and soon crosses an open, dolomite glade. Open woodland birds, such as northern flickers, blue jays, northern cardinals, dark-eyed juncos and American goldfinches favor this area. Entering the forest, the trail descends to a stream where the second loop leads across another ridge (see map). This secluded woodland is a good place to find woodpeckers, titmice, nuthatches, chickadees and an occasional barred owl. The eastern end of the loop provides a broad view of the lake and another opportunity to look for ospreys. Complete the second loop and then finish the first loop as it meanders eastward along an inlet; watch for belted kingfishers in this area.

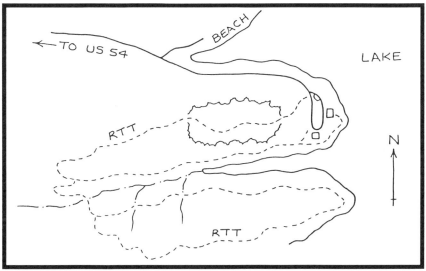

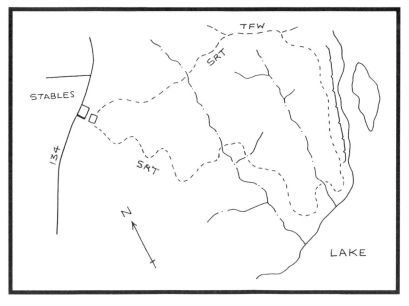

JOURNEY TO THE SUN
OCTOBER-NOVEMBER

While many bird species migrate to southern climes for the winter, it is the waterfowl that have inspired man's wanderlust over the centuries. Their relatively large size, gregarious nature and vocal exhortations all combine to stir even the most urban-minded observers.

Waterfowl migration peaks from mid October through November as large flocks of geese and ducks appear on Midwestern lakes. Joining them are smaller groups of swans, loons, pelicans and grebes, creating an annual rush for birders. Mingling with the waterfowl are migrant gulls, terns and late shorebirds, all wary of peregrine falcons and bald eagles that follow these autumn travellers.

Such spectacles unfold on many lakes and reservoirs across Missouri. I suggest a trip to three areas north of Kansas City: Little Bean Marsh, Smithville Lake and Cooley Lake. These areas provide an excellent overview of wetland habitat. **Little Bean Marsh**, as its name implies, is a broad, open marshland on the Missouri River floodplain, laced with bottomland woods, ponds and sloughs. **Smithville Lake** is a large, man-made reservoir, which attracts a superb variety of diving birds (ducks, mergansers, loons, grebes and cormorants) as well as those that fish from above (ospreys and bald eagles). Finally, **Cooley Lake** is a shallow, oxbow wetland on the Missouri River floodplain, which is a magnet for coot, surface-feeding ducks and pied-billed grebes.

Directions: From I-29 at Platte City, take Exit 20. Follow Missouri 273 north for 16 miles to the Little Bean Marsh entry road, on your left; this entrance will be approximately 3 miles north of Iatan, Missouri.

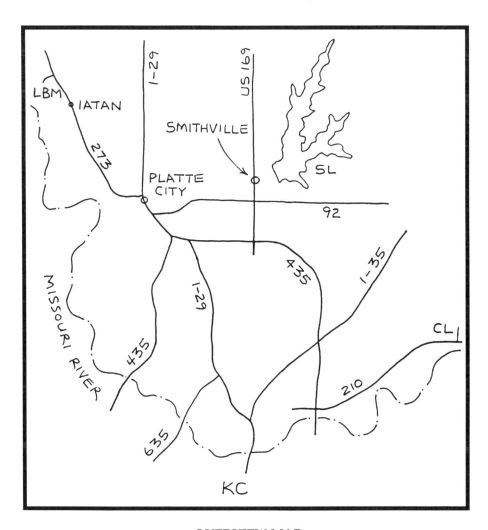

**OVERVIEW MAP
OCTOBER-NOVEMBER FIELD TRIP**

LBM - LITTLE BEAN MARSH
SVL   SMITHVILLE LAKE
CL - COOLEY LAKE

LITTLE BEAN MARSH NATURAL HISTORY AREA

Purchased by the Missouri Department of Conservation in 1981, this 430 acre preserve stretches north from Bean Lake on the Missouri River flood-plain. A mosaic of open marshland, fields, sloughs, ponds and bottomland forest, the refuge attracts an excellent variety of birdlife throughout the year. Summer residents include marsh wrens, soras, common yellowthroats, green-backed herons and prothonotary warblers while shorebirds and waders can be abundant here during migrations.

October brings flocks of waterfowl to Little Bean Marsh and the floodplain woodlands come alive with the industry of winter residents. Red-bellied woodpeckers, yellow-rumped warblers, black-capped chickadees, northern cardinals, white-breasted nuthatches and dark-eyed juncos are among the more conspicuous species while Carolina wrens, swamp sparrows, golden-crowned kinglets and American tree sparrows can also be found. The floodplain woodlands and thickets at Little Bean Marsh are among the better areas in Missouri to find Lincoln's sparrows, Harris' sparrows and winter wrens. Watch also for barred owls, which roost in the larger trees.

Out on the open fields and marshlands, a variety of raptors patrol the landscape. Northern harriers, rough-legged hawks, American kestrels and red-tailed hawks are all common here. Bald eagles also winter at the refuge, congregating near the river and lakes.

The wetland is accessed by two paved trails which diverge just north of the parking lot. The longer, western segment ends at a tower (T) which over-looks the open marsh and provides a distant view of Little Bean Lake. The shorter, eastern arm leads to a blind (B) on Cottonwood Slough (see map).

Directions: After exploring Little Bean Marsh, backtrack on Missouri 273 to I-29 and head south. Take Exit 18 and drive east on Missouri 92. Proceed 12 miles, crossing over U.S. 169, and turn left (north) on Route DD. The **Visitor Center** for **Smithville Lake** will be 1.3 miles ahead, on your right.

Cottonwood Slough

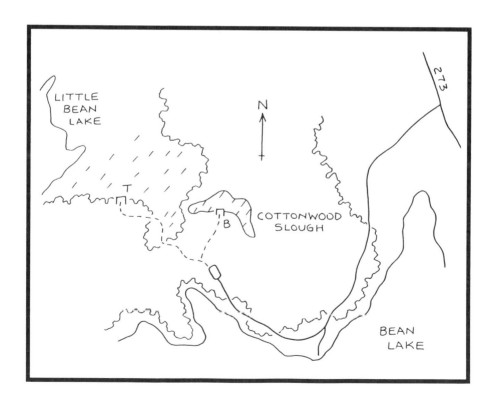

SMITHVILLE LAKE

Impounded by the U.S. Army Corps of Engineers from 1979-1982, this 7190 acre reservoir was created for flood-control, water-supply and recreational purposes; it is now a popular destination for boaters, fishermen and campers. Numerous recreational facilities surround the southern end of the lake and are heavily utilized during the warmer months of the year. By mid-October, the golf and picnic crowds have disappeared and the open waters become a magnet for migrating waterfowl.

Deeper waters, near the **Dam and Visitor Center**, attract common loons, horned grebes and diving ducks; the latter include ring-necked ducks, lesser scaup, common goldeneyes, buffleheads, ruddy ducks and common mergansers. Uncommon visitors include eared grebes, redheads, canvasbacks and red-breasted mergansers. Smithville Lake is also well-known to birders for its rare migrants, including red-throated and Pacific loons, western and Clark's grebes, greater scaup, oldsquaws, surf scoters and white-winged scoters. Joining these deep-water waterfowl are bald eagles, ospreys, Franklin's gulls, ring-billed gulls and migrant terns which fish on the open lake. Birders will appreciate having a spotting scope when viewing these species; a large lawn east of the Visitor Center (VC) and a parking area at the north end of the Dam offer the best vantage points.

The **Honker Cove Waterfowl Refuge (HCWR)** is a 2200 acre protected zone, just north of the Route W bridge. It is best viewed from the boat-ramp at the west end of the bridge, from **access area 1**, at the end of King Road or from **access area 16**, at the end of Road 208 (see map); sectional road mileages are noted. Drowed trees near the center of this refuge fill with huge flocks of double-crested cormorants, which fish in the surrounding waters. Gulls and red-headed woodpeckers also utilize these drowned woodlands and hooded mergansers fish the sheltered coves. Flocks of migrant geese and white pelicans gather near the shorelines, joined by mixed flocks of coot, mallards and other surface-feeding ducks.

Fields and farmlands surrounding the lake offer prime habitat for northern harriers, red-tailed hawks, American kestrels and rough-legged hawks. Watch for northern bobwhites, eastern and western meadowlarks, horned larks, eastern bluebirds and an occasional ring-necked pheasant along the roadways.

Directions: From Smithville Lake, follow U.S. 169 south to I-435 and head east. Proceed to Exit 55 (just past the Amusement Park) and turn left (east) on Missouri 210. Drive 17.5 miles, undulating across the edge of the Missouri River floodplain, and turn left (north) on Route N. Proceed .5 mile and turn left (west) on NE 84th St. Follow this road as it zig-zags back to the edge of Cooley Lake (see map, page 71).

*Backwater shallows
at Smithville Lake*

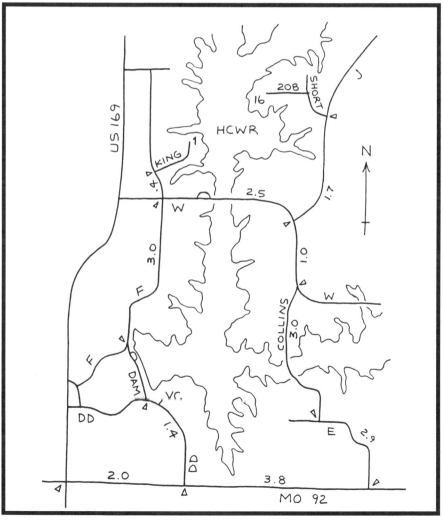

COOLEY LAKE CONSERVATION AREA

This 1348 acre Conservation Area is best known to birders for its 335 acre oxbow lake, which attracts an excellent variety of waterfowl during the spring and fall migrations. The lake is complemented by surrounding marsh, crop fields and floodplain woodlands.

Relatively shallow, the open waters and marsh of Cooley Lake offer ideal feeding habitat for pied-billed grebes, American coot and surface-feeding ducks. Coot are abundant here in October-November, joined by smaller flocks of northern pintail, American wigeon, gadwall, mallards, northern shovelers and green-winged teal.

A graveled drive runs along the east side of the lake, permitting observation from your car (a useful blind). North of the parking area, a wide path follows the curve of the oxbow, passing through bottomland woods and along the edge of a cropfield. Thickets and groves of small trees offer natural blinds for observing the waterfowl and attract a host of winter residents; watch for yellow-rumped warblers, winter wrens, fox sparrows and a variety of more common species in these woodlands.

Northern harriers and red-tailed hawks patrol the open areas and you may spot a great-horned owl among the lakeside timber. Peregrine falcons are uncommon but regular visitors to Cooley Lake, preying on the numerous waterfowl.

Cooley Lake

Woodlands provide a natural blind along the Lake

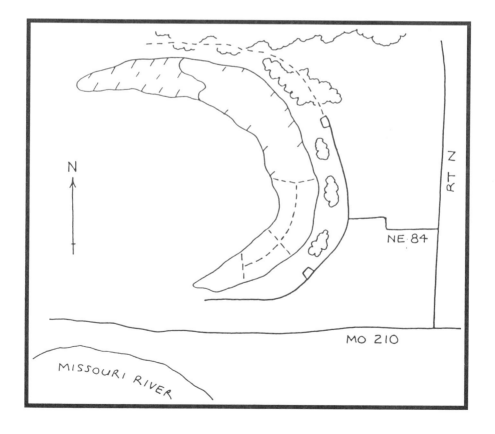

A BLIZZARD OF SNOWS
NOVEMBER-DECEMBER

SQUAW CREEK NATIONAL WILDLIFE REFUGE

Even those who have had the opportunity to visit nature preserves across this varied country will always remember a late autumn visit to the Squaw Creek National Wildlife Refuge, in northwest Missouri. As the November days shorten, some 300,000 snow geese descend on the refuge, joined by large flocks of Canada geese and lesser numbers of greater white-fronted and Ross' geese. Tundra swans and sandhill cranes also visit Squaw Creek and over 100,000 ducks rest and feed here during migrations. Attracted by these spectacular concentrations of waterfowl, as many as 300 bald eagles stop by to feast on the sick and injured birds.

Established in 1935 to provide shallow wetlands across the Missouri River floodplain, this 7178 acre preserve attracts the migrant waterfowl with shallow lakes, marshlands, cropfields and wet meadows. Bottomland timber and loess cliffs add to the natural diversity, drawing over 300 bird species to the refuge in the course of a year. Access to this exciting area is provided by a **10-mile auto tour road (ATR)** and by several field trails. As is often the case when viewing waterfowl, staying within your car permits close approach without disturbing the wildlife.

In addition to the fabulous concentrations of waterfowl and bald eagles, November-December visitors are likely to see northern harriers, short-eared owls and sharp-shinned hawks; this refuge is also a good place to look for rare winter visitors such as prairie falcons, merlins, northern goshawks golden eagles and long-eared owls. Ring-necked pheasants, horned larks and northern bobwhites are often spotted along the roadways and birders should check the brushy fields for American tree sparrows, Harris' sparrows and white-crowned sparrows. Rare winter visitors include northern shrikes, common redpolls, Brewer's blackbirds and Lapland longspurs.

It should be mentioned that the Squaw Creek NWR is also an excellent place to visit during the spring and late summer migrations. Shorebirds are often abundant here and large flocks of American white pelicans visit the refuge at those times. Other common migrants include double-crested cormorants, horned grebes, Franklin's gulls, black terns, soras, American coot and Forster's terns. American bitterns, least bitterns, great egrets, little blue herons, black-crowned night herons and yellow-headed blackbirds are among the summer residents.

The mammal population at Squaw Creek includes white-tailed deer, red fox, coyote, beaver, muskrat, cottontails and meadow voles. The endangered massasauga rattlesnake also inhabits the preserve.

Directions: From I-29, south of Mound City, take Exit 79 and head west on U.S. 159, soon descending onto the Missouri River floodplain. The **Visitor Center (VC)** will be on your left while the **Auto Tour Road (ATR)** will be on your right. The refuge is open daily, from sunrise to sunset.

*A view across
the marsh*

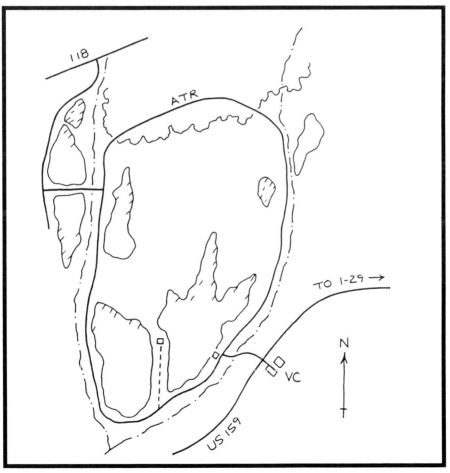

VISITORS FROM THE NORTH
DECEMBER-JANUARY

RIVERLANDS ENVIRONMENTAL DEMONSTRATION AREA

Gulls are opportunistic creatures. Ring-billed and herring gulls, the two most common species in Missouri, have learned to supplement their diet of fish by scavenging at garbage dumps and fast food parking lots. They have also learned to congregate around locks and dams, where they can glean stunned fish from the turbulent waters.

Such is the case at the **Melvin Price Locks and Dam** on the Mississippi, just downstream from Alton, Illinois. Joining the common gulls are a superb variety of other winter visitors, including greater and lesser black-backed, glaucous and Thayer's gulls. On the deep waters behind the Dam, huge flocks of canvasbacks, common goldeneyes and common mergansers gather to rest and feed; they are joined by lesser numbers of redheads, ring-necked ducks, and buffleheads. Rare visitors, such as oldsquaws, surf scoters, black scoters, white-winged scoters, black-legged kittiwakes and Barrow's goldeneyes may also be found; during the winter of 2000-2001, a smew appeared on the scene, the first ever observed in Missouri.

Adjoining the west bank of the Mississippi is the **Riverlands Environmental Demonstration Area**, established in 1988. This 1200 acre refuge, characterized by shallow wetlands, meadows, crop fields and bottomland timber, is accessed by a network of roadways (see map); visitors are asked to stay on these roads and parking areas from October 15 to April 15, ensuring safe refuge for the wintering waterfowl. Huge flocks of Canada geese winter here, joined by mixed flocks of mallards, American black ducks, green-winged teal, gadwall, northern pintail and American wigeon. Tundra and trumpeter swans, snow geese and greater white-fronted geese may also be found.

Overseeing these spectacular concentrations of waterfowl are a large number of bald eagles; look for them in the riverside trees or perched on man-made structures near the Dam. Check the open fields for northern harriers, rough-legged hawks, red-tailed hawks and short-eared owls. Other winter residents include peregrine falcons, horned larks, Lapland longspurs, white-crowned sparrows, American tree sparrows, golden-crowned kinglets, rusty blackbirds, ring-necked pheasants and northern bobwhites. Snow buntings may visit during severe winters and long-eared owls are occasionally found in the wooded areas.

Directions: From I-270 on the north side of St. Louis, take Exit 31 and head north on Route 367 which will soon merge with U.S. 67. Turn northeast on U.S. 67 (toward Alton, Illinois), cross the Missouri River and continue past West Alton. The entry road for the Riverlands Environmental Demonstration Area will be on your right, a short distance before reaching the Mississippi River bridge (see map).

Ellis Bay Waterfowl Refuge

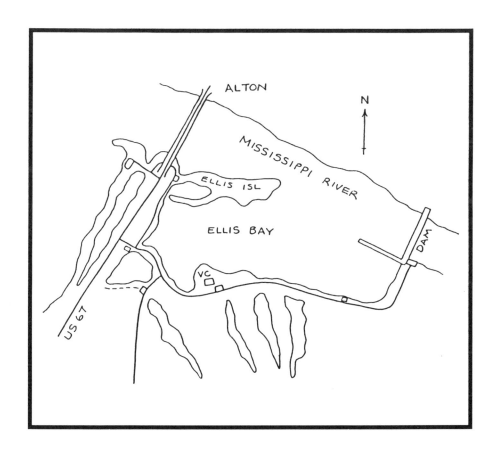

WINTER IN THE COUNTRY
JANUARY

Novice birders and naturalists often shun winter field trips, confining their excursions to the pleasant months of April to October. This is unfortunate in several respects. Many bird species are only found in Missouri during the winter months and many permanent residents, such as woodpeckers and owls, tend to be more conspicuous in the barren forest. In addition, non-hibernating mammals are often more active, and thus more visible, during the colder months. If nothing else, a journey into the woods or fields on a crisp winter day is a good cure for cabin fever.

I suggest a January visit to three nature preserves in central Missouri which provide an overview of the winter landscape and ensure exposure to a good variety of permanent and winter residents. The **C.W. Green Conservation Area** is an environmental research area, south of Columbia, which offers a mix of marsh-lined ponds, open fields and upland woods. **Bradford Farm**, south-east of Columbia, is an Agricultural Research Station of the University of Missouri; it is characterized by open grasslands and crop fields. Finally, the **Little Dixie Lake Conservation Area**, in Callaway County, harbors a mix of forest and field, centered around a 205 acre lake.

Directions: From Columbia, head south on U.S. 63. Pass the Exit for the Columbia Regional Airport (Route H) and continue another 1.5 miles and turn right (west) on Minor Hill Road. The Charles W. Green Conservation Area will be .25 mile ahead, on your right.

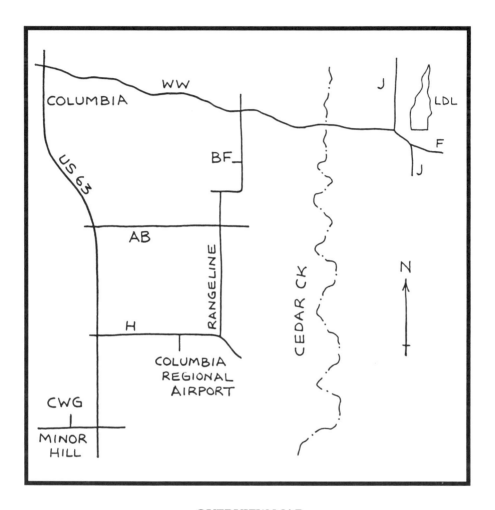

OVERVIEW MAP
JANUARY FIELD TRIP

CWG - CHARLES W. GREEN C.A.
BF - BRADFORD FARM
LDL - LITTLE DIXIE LAKE C.A.

CHARLES W. GREEN CONSERVATION AREA

This little known and sparsely utilized Environmental Research area offers a peaceful escape in mid winter. Park near the headquarters building (HQ) and stroll westward to the complex of ponds (see map). This is a good area to find swamp and song sparrows, occasionally joined by lingering migrants such as Lincoln's sparrows. Scan the winter sky and woodland borders for red-tailed, sharp-shinned and rough-legged hawks, American kestrels and northern harriers.

Follow the central roadway as it leads northward, passing meadows, crop fields, ponds, shrubby woodlands and parcels of forest. Northern bobwhites, horned larks and dark-eyed juncos often feed along the graveled road and the open meadows attract field sparrows, eastern meadowlarks, eastern bluebirds and mourning doves. American crows are among the more conspicuous residents, noisily moving about the preserve. Check thickets and wood margins for American tree and fox sparrows, golden-crowned kinglets, hermit thrushes, northern cardinals, American goldfinches and possible winter wrens. Cedar groves attract American robins, northern mockingbirds and cedar waxwings and may harbor a roosting northern saw-whet owl.

Wooded areas are the domain of northern flickers, red-bellied, hairy and downy woodpeckers, yellow-bellied sapsuckers, tufted titmice, brown creepers, black-capped chickadees, white-breasted and red-breasted nuthatches, blue jays and eastern screech owls. A visit at dusk may turn up a great horned owl as it departs the forest for a night of hunting.

At the north end of the roadway, a jeep trail circles down through the forested valley of Bass Creek. Complete this loop and then return to your car via the central road.

Directions: From the Charles W. Green Conservation Area, return to U.S. 63 and head north. Take the Exit for the Columbia Regional Airport and drive east on Route H. Proceed almost 2 miles and turn left (north) on Rangeline Road. Continue on this road for 4.8 miles to the **Bradford Farm** entrance, on your left; note that Rangeline Road jogs to the east enroute (see overview map, page 77).

A brisk day at the Charles W. Green refuge

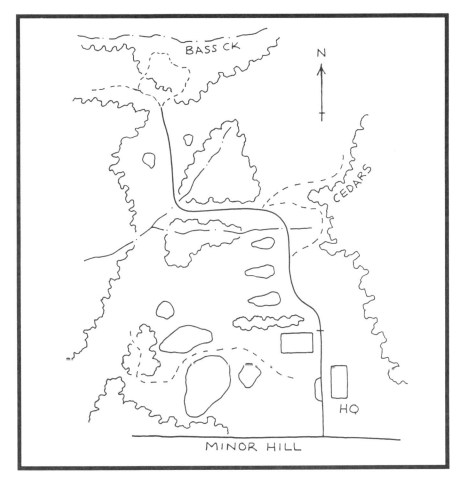

BRADFORD FARM

This agricultural research center, operated by the University of Missouri, attracts an interesting mix of open-country birds during the winter months. Broad grasslands and crop fields offer prime habitat for voles and mice, the favored prey of many raptors. Northern harriers, red-tailed hawks, northern rough-legged hawks and American kestrels are all common here. It is one of the better places in Missouri to observe short eared owls; these diurnal predators are often spotted sitting on a low branch, or directly on the ground, oblivious to the cold and snow. Bradford Farm is also known as a good spot to look for rare winter visitors such as prairie falcons, merlins and snowy owls.

In addition to the raptors, winter birders should also find eastern and western meadowlarks, Canada geese, horned larks, eastern bluebirds, Lapland and Smith's longspurs, white-crowned sparrows and, in severe winters, snow buntings. Watch for loggerhead shrikes that usually hunt from fence posts or saplings, and check the thickets and brushpiles for Harris' sparrows.

Directions: After exploring the farm, return to Rangeline Road and turn left (north). Drive 2 miles and turn right (east) on Route WW. Proceed 4.5 miles into Millersburg, where WW intersects Route J; the Little Dixie Lake Conservation Area is just northeast of this junction (see map, page 83).

*Open grassland and cropfields attract a superb
variety of raptors to Bradford Farm*

A refuge from the winter wind

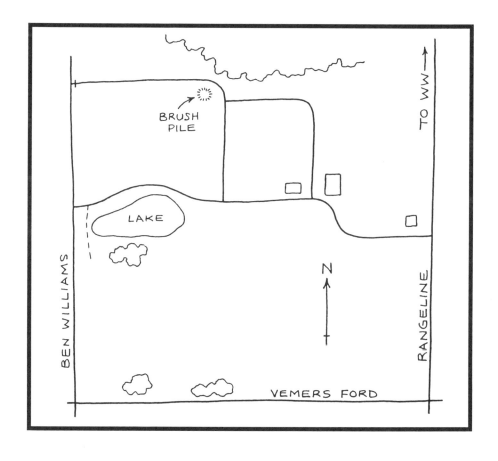

LITTLE DIXIE LAKE CONSERVATION AREA

Located in western Callaway County, between Columbia and Fulton, the Little Dixie Lake Conservation Area is a popular destination for fishermen. Seasonal hunting is also permitted across the northern half of the preserve.

In most winters, the lake's deeper waters remain open, attracting large flocks of Canada geese and a mixed assembly of gulls and ducks. Common loons turn up on a regular basis, especially during migrations, and winter visitors include such rare species as white-winged scoters. A few bald eagles are usually found here from November to March, feeding on fish and injured waterfowl. All of these deep water species are best viewed from the Dam or from the southwest and southeast parking lots (see map).

The **Shoreline (S)** and **Boundary (B) Trails** provide access to woodlands and fields that surround the lake. Small meadows along the west side of the Conservation Area are especially good for wintering sparrows: field, song, swamp, fox, American tree, white-throated and white-crowned sparrows should be found. They are joined by American goldfinches, house finches, northern cardinals and dark-eyed juncos.

Woodlands east of the lake offer prime habitat for woodpeckers (all seven of Missouri's species), Cooper's hawks, titmice, chickadees, nuthatches, brown creepers, yellow-rumped warblers, hermit thrushes, wild turkeys and owls (eastern screech, great horned and barred). Check stands of cedar for northern mockingbirds, cedar waxwings and a possible northern saw-whet owl.

Winter grips the refuge

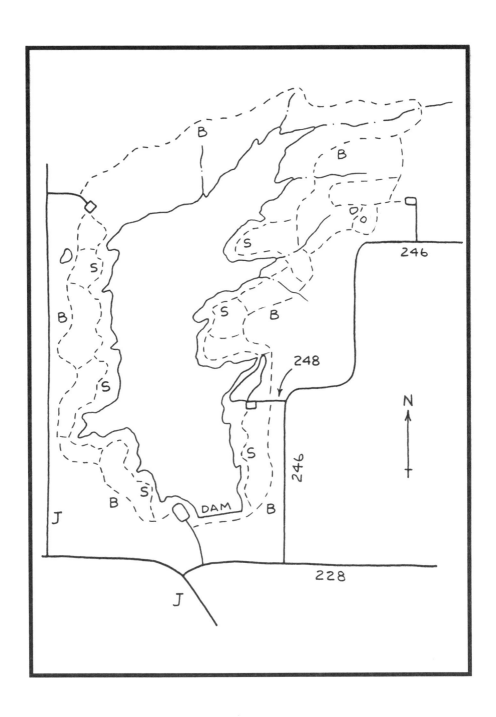

MISSOURI'S GREAT LAKES
FEBRUARY

A chain of large reservoirs, all part of the Osage River watershed, high-lights the map of southwest Missouri. Even during the most severe winters, the deep waters of these lakes remain open, attracting a mix of loons, diving ducks, gulls and eagles. Among the more regular visitors are common loons, common goldeneyes, buffleheads, lesser scaup, redheads, ring-necked ducks, common mergansers, ring-billed gulls and bald eagles. Patient observers may also find rare visitors such as Pacific, yellow-billed and red-throated loons, white-winged, surf and black scoters, pomarine and parasitic jaegers, Thay-er's and glaucous gulls and greater scaup. Flocks of Canada geese generally winter at the reservoirs and surrounding farmlands attract raptors such as northern harriers, northern rough-legged hawks, red-tailed hawks and short-eared owls.

A combined field trip to **Truman Reservoir**, **Pomme de Terre Lake** and **Stockton Lake** is outlined below. Plan to bring warm, layered clothing, high energy snacks, a thermos of hot chocholate, tea or coffee and, if available, a good spotting scope.

Directions: From U.S. 65 on the north side of Warsaw, exit west toward the Truman Lake Dam and Visitor Center; the latter will be approximately 1.25 miles west of U.S. 65 and the Dam will be a short distance further. The deep lake waters are best viewed from a lot at the Project Headquarters Building (HQ), at the south end of the Dam.

Pomme de Terre Lake

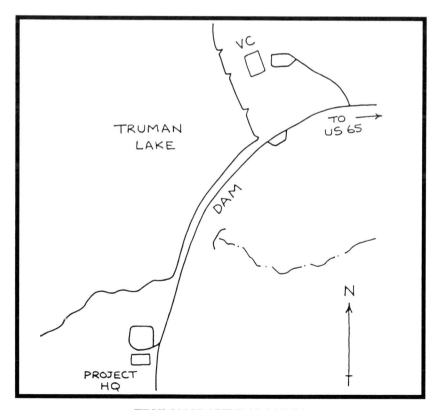

TRUMAN LAKE DAM AREA

Directions:

After visiting Truman Lake, return to U.S. 65 and head south to the junction with U.S. 54. Turn right (west) on U.S. 54 and drive 6 miles to Hermitage. Turn left (south) on 254/64 toward **Pomme de Terre Lake**. Proceed 3 miles and bear right onto 254. The Damsite Park entrance will be .3 miles ahead, on your left while lots at the Dam itself will be 1 mile ahead. The deep waters adjacent to the Dam can be viewed from either area.

Directions:

From Pomme de Terre Lake, head west on 254 to Missouri 83. Turn left (south) and follow this route as it zigzags down to Bolivar. Turn right (west) on Missouri 32, cross Missouri 13, and drive 18.4 miles to the **Crabtree Cove (CC)** access for **Stockton Lake**; the **Damsite** roadway will be another 1.5 miles on Missouri 32.

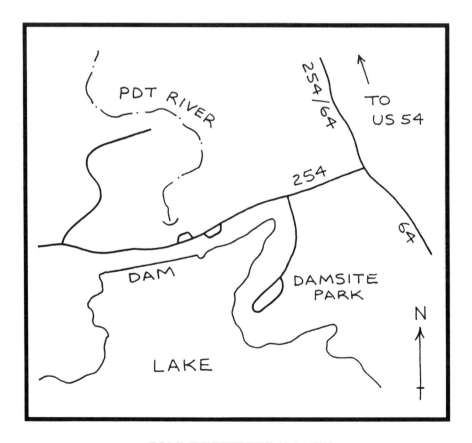

POMME DE TERRE DAM AREA

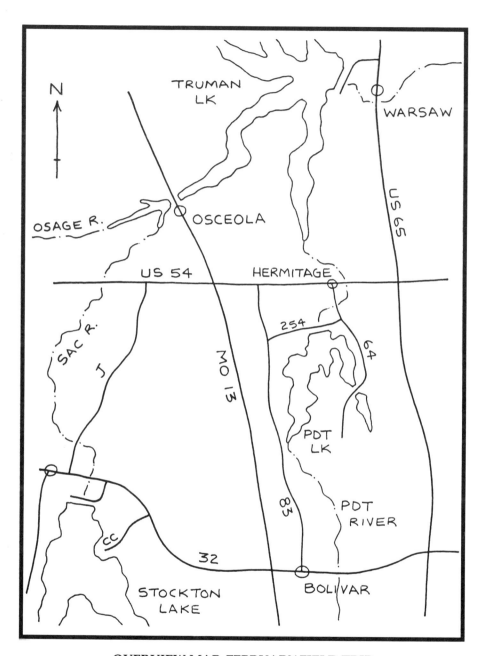

OVERVIEW MAP: FEBRUARY FIELD TRIP

IV. THE BIRDS OF MISSOURI

This Chapter provides a checklist of Missouri birds, grouped by family. For each species, the following information is provided:

Status: Indicates whether that bird is abundant, common, uncommon or rare in Missouri and whether it is a permanent resident, seasonal resident, seasonal visitor or migrant in our State. Very rare or "accidental" species are not included.

> **Abundant** - easily found in that bird's preferred habitat
> **Common** - usually found in that bird's preferred habitat
> **Uncommon** - generally found about half the time
> **Rare** - not likely to be found on most field trips
> **Locally common or abundant** - rare or uncommon throughout most of Missouri but concentrated in certain areas of the State
> **Erratic** - numbers vary widely from year to year

> **Permanent Resident** - found in Missouri throughout the year
> **Summer Resident** - returns to Missouri in the spring, breeds here and then leaves for wintering grounds in the fall
> **Winter Resident** - winters in Missouri from autumn to mid spring
> **Summer and Winter visitors** - wander into the State during these general seasons; summer visitors are usually best found in August or September
> **Migrant** - passes through Missouri on its way between summer and winter ranges, stopping to rest and feed in our State

Habitat: Indicates that bird's preferred habitat. Some birds, such as Canada geese, can be found in a variety of habitats through the course of a day. The primary habitats of Missouri include:

> **Deep lakes and rivers** - favored by loons, diving ducks, bald eagles and ospreys
> **Shallow lakes and wetlands** - the preferred habitat of geese, most ducks, waders, pelicans, rails, coot and shorebirds
> **Riparian woodlands** - moist woods along streams and lakeshores; favored by kingfishers, barred owls, red-headed woodpeckers and a variety of songbirds
> **Forest and woodlots** - home to a large number of songbirds, owls, jays, wild turkeys and woodpeckers
> **Immature woodlands and thickets** - the chosen habitat of cardinals, wrens, sparrows and finches
> **Grasslands and meadows** - the domain of raptors, vultures, bluebirds, horned larks, meadowlarks, northern bobwhites and longspurs

Recommendation: A specific area and time of year for observing each species is suggested. For abundant or common residents that are found throughout Missouri, the designation of "widespread" is made.

The recommendation is based on my own observations as well as on data supplied by the various nature preserves. When visiting an area with the hope of finding a specific bird species, I suggest that you stop by the visitor center or park office to ask the naturalist about recent sightings.

LOONS & GREBES

___**Common Loon**
> Status: Uncommon migrant; locally common
> Habitat: Deep lakes and rivers
> Recommendation: Smithville Lake, November

___**Yellow-billed Loon**
> Status: Rare winter visitor and migrant
> Habitat: Deep lakes and rivers
> Recommendation: Stockton Lake, winter

___**Pacific Loon**
>   Status: Rare winter visitor and migrant
>   Habitat: Deep lakes and rivers
>   Recommendation: Smithville Lake, November-December

___**Red-throated Loon**
>   Status: Rare migrant
>   Habitat: Deep lakes and rivers
>   Recommendation: Smithville Lake, November-December

___**Clark's Grebe:**
>   Status: Rare migrant
>   Habitat: Deep lakes and rivers
>   Recommendation: Smithville Lake, October-November

___**Western Grebe**
>   Status: Uncommon migrant in western Missouri
>   Habitat: Deep lakes and rivers
>   Recommendation: Squaw Creek NWR, October-November

___**Red-necked Grebe**
>   Status: Rare migrant
>   Habitat: Deep lakes and rivers
>   Recommendation: Ted Shanks C.A., October-November

___**Horned Grebe**
>   Status: Uncommon migrant
>   Habitat: Deep lakes and rivers
>   Recommendation: Riverlands Demo Area, March or November

___**Eared Grebe**
>   Status: Uncommon migrant, primarily in western Missouri
>   Habitat: Deep lakes and rivers
>   Recommendation: Squaw Creek NWR, April or October

___**Pied-billed Grebe**
>   Status: Common migrant; uncommon summer resident; permanent
>   resident in southeast Missouri
>   Habitat: Shallow lakes and wetlands
>   Recommendation: Cooley Lake, October

PELICANS, CORMORANTS & ANHINGAS

___American White Pelican
> Status: Common migrant; uncommon summer visitor
> Habitat: Shallow lakes and wetlands
> Recommendation: Squaw Creek NWR, September

___Double-crested Cormorant
> Status: Common migrant; rare to uncommon summer resident; locally
>   uncommon to common winter resident
> Habitat: Deep lakes and rivers
> Recommendation: Smithville Lake, October-November

___Anhinga
> Status: Rare summer visitor in southeast Missouri
> Habitat: Lakes and rivers
> Recommendation: Mingo NWR, summer

HERONS, BITTERNS & EGRETS

___Least Bittern
> Status: Uncommon summer resident
> Habitat: Shallow lakes and wetlands
> Recommendation: Ted Shanks C.A., May-June

___American Bittern
> Status: Uncommon summer resident
> Habitat: Shallow lakes and wetlands
> Recommendation: Mingo NWR, May

___Black-crowned Night Heron
> Status: Common summer resident
> Habitat: Shallow lakes and wetlands
> Recommendation: Clarence Cannon NWR, May-June

*Black-crowned
Night Heron*

*Photo by
Sherm Spoelstra*

___**Yellow-crowned Night Heron**
Status: Uncommon summer resident
Habitat: Shallow lakes and wetlands
Recommendation: Mingo NWR, May-September

___**Green-backed Heron**
Status: Common summer resident
Habitat: Shallow lakes and wetlands
Recommendation: Ted Shanks C.A., May-September

___**Little Blue Heron**
Status: Uncommon summer visitor; summer resident in southeast
Habitat: Shallow lakes and wetlands
Recommendation: Mingo NWR, May

___**Cattle Egret**
Status: Uncommon migrant and summer visitor; summer resident in
southeast Missouri
Habitat: Grasslands and wetlands
Recommendation: Mingo NWR, May; Ted Shanks C.A. & vicinity,
September

___**Snowy Egret**
>Status: Rare summer visitor and local summer resident in southeast
>Habitat: Shallow lakes and wetlands
>Recommendation: Clarence Cannon NWR, August-September

___**Great Egret**
>Status: Common summer resident; locally abundant
>Habitat: Shallow lakes and wetlands
>Recommendation: Ted Shanks C.A. and Clarence Cannon NWR,
>   May-September; Eagle Bluffs C.A., August-September

___**Great Blue Heron**
>Status: Common summer resident; locally abundant; uncommon
>   permanent resident throughout much of Missouri
>Habitat: Shallow lakes and wetlands
>Recommendation: Eagle Bluffs C.A., April-September

IBIS & SPOONBILLS

___**Glossy Ibis**
>Status: Rare summer visitor in southeast Missouri
>Habitat: Shallow lakes and wetlands
>Recommendation: Otter Slough C.A., late summer

___**White-faced Ibis**
>Status: Uncommon migrant and rare summer visitor
>Habitat: Shallow lakes and wetlands
>Recommendation: Eagle Bluffs C.A., May

White-faced Ibis

*Photo by Sherm
Spoelstra*

___White Ibis
>   Status: Rare summer visitor along Mississippi River
>   Habitat: Shallow lakes and wetlands
>   Recommendation: Big Oak Tree State Park & vicinity; summer

___Roseate Spoonbill
>   Status: Rare and erratic summer visitor in southeast Missouri
>   Habitat: Shallow lakes and wetlands
>   Recommendation: Mingo NWR, summer

CRANES

___Sandhill Crane
>   Status: Rare migrant, primarily in northwestern Missouri
>   Habitat: Grasslands and wetlands
>   Recommendation: Squaw Creek NWR, October-November

SWANS, GEESE & DUCKS

___Tundra Swan
>   Status: Rare migrant; locally uncommon
>   Habitat: Shallow lakes and wetlands; rivers
>   Recommendation: Squaw Creek NWR, November; Mingo NWR,
>   winter

___Trumpeter Swan
>   Status: Rare; undergoing reintroduction in the Midwest
>   Habitat: Shallow lakes and wetlands; rivers
>   Recommendation: Riverlands Demo Area, November-December;
>   Mingo NWR, winter

___Greater White-Fronted Goose
>   Status: Uncommon migrant
>   Habitat: Grasslands and wetlands
>   Recommendation: Squaw Creek NWR, November

___Snow Goose
>   Status: Common migrant; locally abundant
>   Habitat: Grasslands and wetlands
>   Recommendation: Squaw Creek NWR, November-December

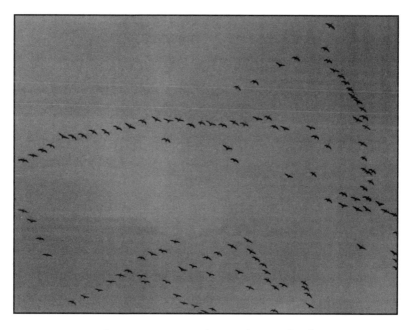

Snow geese returning to Squaw Creek

___**Ross' Goose**
>Status: Rare migrant; locally uncommon
>Habitat: Grasslands and wetlands
>Recommendation: Squaw Creek NWR, November

___**Canada Goose**
>Status: Common permanent resident; locally abundant, especially
>during migrations and winter months
>Habitat: Grasslands and wetlands
>Recommendation: Swan Lake NWR, November-March; Riverlands
>Demonstration Area, winter

___**Brant**
>Status: Rare migrant
>Habitat: Grasslands and wetlands
>Recommendation: Squaw Creek NWR, November

___**Mallard**
>Status: Abundant permanent resident
>Habitat: Shallow lakes and wetlands
>Recommendation: Widespread

___**Amerian Black Duck**
     Status: Uncommon winter resident; locally common
     Habitat: Shallow lakes and wetlands
     Recommendation: Mingo NWR, winter

___**Gadwall**
     Status: Common migrant and winter resident
     Habitat: Shallow lakes and wetlands
     Recommendation: Otter Slough C.A., April; Cooley Lake,
        November

___**Green-winged Teal**
     Status: Common migrant and winter resident
     Habitat: Shallow lakes and wetlands
     Recommendation: Squaw Creek NWR or Riverlands Demo Area,
        November and March

___**American Wigeon**
     Status: Common migrant; locally uncommon winter resident
     Habitat: Shallow lakes and wetlands
     Recommendation: Grand Pass C.A., March; Cooley Lake, October

___**Northern Pintail**
     Status: Uncommon migrant and winter resident; locally common
     Habitat: Shallow lakes and wetlands
     Recommendation: Grand Pass C.A., March; Cooley Lake, November

___**Northern Shoveler**
     Status: Common migrant and uncommon winter resident; summer
        resident in northern Missouri
     Habitat: Shallow lakes and wetlands
     Recommendation: Otter Slough C.A., April

___**Blue-winged Teal**
     Status: Common summer resident; abundant migrant
     Habitat: Shallow lakes and wetlands
     Recommendation: Eagle Bluffs C.A. or Otter Slough C.A., April

___**Cinnamon Teal**
     Status: Rare migrant in western Missouri
     Habitat: Shallow lakes and wetlands
     Recommendation: Squaw Creek NWR, September

___**Ruddy Duck**
>   Status: Uncommon migrant and winter resident
>   Habitat: Deep lakes and rivers
>   Recommendation: Smithville Lake or Riverlands Demo Area,
>   October-November

___**Wood Duck**
>   Status: Common permanent resident
>   Habitat: Wooded ponds, streams and backwaters
>   Recommendation: Mingo NWR, April-May

Male Wood Duck   (photo by Sherm Spoelstra)

___**Canvasback**
>   Status: Uncommon migrant; locally common winter resident
>   Habitat: Deep lakes and rivers
>   Recommendation: Riverlands Demo Area, winter

___**Redhead**
>   Status: Uncommon migrant and winter resident; locally common
>   Habitat: Deep lakes and rivers
>   Recommendation: Swan Lake NWR, March

___**Ring-necked Duck**
>   Status: Common migrant and winter resident .
>   Habitat: Deep lakes and rivers
>   Recommendation: Fountain Grove C.A., March

___Greater Scaup
> Status: Rare migrant
> Habitat: Deep lakes and rivers
> Recommendation: Smithville Lake, November-December

___Lesser Scaup
> Status: Common migrant and winter resident
> Habitat: Deep lakes and rivers
> Recommendation: Fountain Grove C.A., March; Smithville Lake,
> November

___Black Scoter
> Status: Rare migrant and winter visitor
> Habitat: Deep lakes and rivers
> Recommendation: Riverlands Demo Area, winter

___White-winged Scoter
> Status: Rare migrant and winter visitor
> Habitat: Deep lakes and rivers
> Recommendation: Riverlands Demo Area or Smithville Lake,
> winter

___Surf Scoter
> Status: Rare migrant and winter visitor
> Habitat: Deep lakes and rivers
> Recommendation: Riverlands Demo Area or Smithville Lake,
> winter

___Oldsquaw
> Status: Rare winter visitor
> Habitat: Deep lakes and rivers
> Recommendation: Riverlands Demo Area, winter

___Common Goldeneye
> Status: Common winter resident
> Habitat: Deep lakes and rivers
> Recommendation: Riverlands Demo Area or Smithville Lake,
> November-March

___Bufflehead
> Status: Common winter resident
> Habitat: Deep lakes and rivers
> Recommendation: Swan Lake NWR, March; Smithville Lake,
> November-December

___Common Merganser
>Status: Uncommon winter resident; locally abundant
>Habitat: Deep lakes and rivers
>Recommendation: Riverlands Demo Area, winter

___Red-breasted Merganser
>Status: Uncommon to rare migrant
>Habitat: Deep lakes and rivers
>Recommendation: Smithville Lake, November

___Hooded Merganser
>Status: Uncommon permanent resident; numbers increase in summer
>Habitat: Wooded ponds, streams and backwaters
>Recommendation: Swan Lake NWR, March

RAILS, MOORHENS & COOT

___King Rail
>Status: Uncommon summer resident
>Habitat: Wetlands
>Recommendation: Ted Shanks C.A., May-June

___Virginia Rail
>Status: Uncommon migrant; summer resident in northern Missouri
>Habitat: Wetlands
>Recommendation: Ted Shanks C.A. or Clarence Cannon NWR,
>   May

___Sora
>Status: Uncommon migrant; summer resident in northern Missouri
>Habitat: Wetlands
>Recommendation: Clarence Cannon NWR, April-June

___Yellow Rail
>Status: Rare migrant
>Habitat: Wetlands
>Recommendation: Squaw Creek NWR, May

___Common Moorhen
>Status: Common summer resident in southeast Missouri; rare in
>   other regions of the State
>Habitat: Shallow lakes and wetlands
>Recommendation: Mingo NWR, May-September

___**American Coot**
Status: Rare to uncommon permanent resident; abundant migrant
Habitat: Shallow lakes and wetlands
Recommendation: Eagle Bluffs C.A. or Otter Slough C.A., April;
Cooley Lake, October

SHOREBIRDS, SNIPE & WOODCOCK

___**American Avocet**
Status: Uncommon migrant
Habitat: Shallow lakes and wetlands
Recommendation: Squaw Creek NWR, May and September

___**Black-necked Stilt**
Status: Rare migrant and summer visitor in Mississippi Valley
Habitat: Shallow lakes and wetlands
Recommendation: Otter Slough C.A. and vicinity, May

___**Snowy Plover**
Status: Rare migrant
Habitat: Lakeshores and mudflats
Recommendation: Squaw Creek NWR, May

___**Piping Plover**
Status: Rare to uncommon migrant
Habitat: Lakeshores and mudflats
Recommendation: Squaw Creek NWR or Ted Shanks C.A., August-
September

___**Semipalmated Plover**
Status: Uncommon migrant
Habitat: Lakeshores and mudflats
Recommendation: Eagle Bluffs C.A., August

___**Killdeer**
Status: Common summer resident; permanent resident in
southeast Missouri
Habitat: Lakeshores, mudflats and grasslands
Recommendation: Eagle Bluffs C.A., April-September

___**Black-bellied Plover**
　　Status: Uncommon migrant
　　Habitat: Lakeshores and mudflats
　　Recommendation: Clarence Cannon NWR, May

___**Lesser Golden Plover**
　　Status: Rare spring migrant
　　Habitat: Mudflats and wet fields
　　Recommendation: Otter Slough C.A., April

___**Marbled Godwit**
　　Status: Rare migrant
　　Habitat: Lakeshores and wet fields
　　Recommendation: Squaw Creek NWR or Riverlands Demo Area,
　　　　September

___**Hudsonian Godwit**
　　Status: Uncommon migrant
　　Habitat: Lakeshores and wet fields
　　Recommendation: Squaw Creek NWR, April-May

___**Whimbrel**
　　Status: Rare migrant
　　Habitat: Lakeshores and wet fields
　　Recommendation: Squaw Creek NWR, May

___**Long-billed Curlew**
　　Status: Rare migrant
　　Habitat: Grasslands and wetlands
　　Recommendation: Squaw Creek NWR, April-May

___**Willet**
　　Status: Rare migrant; locally uncommon
　　Habitat: Lakeshores and mudflats
　　Recommendation: Squaw Creek NWR, May

___**Greater Yellowlegs**
　　Status: Common migrant
　　Habitat: Lakeshores and mudflats
　　Recommendation: Clarence Cannon NWR or Ted Shanks C.A.,
　　　　April-May

Look for shorebirds on backwater beaches and mudflats

___**Lesser Yellowlegs**
> Status: Common migrant; locally abundant
> Habitat: Lakeshores and mudflats
> Recommendation: Clarence Cannon NWR or Ted Shanks C.A.,
> May; Eagle Bluffs C.A., August-September

___**Solitary Sandpiper**
> Status: Uncommon migrant
> Habitat: Lakeshores and mudflats
> Recommendation: Eagle Bluffs C.A., August-September

___**Spotted Sandpiper**
> Status: Common summer resident
> Habitat: Lakeshores, streambanks and wetlands
> Recommendation: Clarence Cannon NWR or Ted Shanks C.A.,
> May-September

___**Wilson's Phalarope**
> Status: Uncommon migrant
> Habitat: Shallow lakes and wetlands
> Recommendation: Squaw Creek NWR, May

___**Red-necked Phalarope**
> Status: Rare migrant
> Habitat: Shallow lakes and wetlands
> Recommendation: Riverlands Demo Area, August-September

___**Short-billed Dowitcher**
>   Status: Uncommon migrant
>   Habitat: Lakeshores and migrants
>   Recommendation: Clarence Cannon NWR or Ted Shanks C.A.,
>   September

___**Long-billed Dowitcher**
>   Status: Uncommon migrant; locally common
>   Habitat: Lakeshores and mudflats
>   Recommendation: Squaw Creek NWR, October

___**Stilt Sandpiper**
>   Status: Uncommon migrant
>   Habitat: Lakeshores and mudflats
>   Recommendation: Riverlands Demo Area, September

___**Common Snipe**
>   Status: Uncommon migrant and winter resident
>   Habitat: Wetlands and streambanks
>   Recommendation: Fountain Grove C.A., March

___**American Woodcock**
>   Status: Common but local summer resident; permanent resident
>   in southeast Missouri
>   Habitat: Wooded swamps and moist, open woodlands
>   Recommendation: Mingo NWR, March-April

___**Ruddy Turnstone**
>   Status: Rare migrant
>   Habitat: Lakeshores and mudflats
>   Recommendation: Squaw Creek NWR, May

___**Red Knot**
>   Status: Rare migrant
>   Habitat: Lakeshores and mudflats
>   Recommendation: Squaw Creek NWR, May

___**Dunlin**
>   Status: Uncommon migrant
>   Habitat: Lakeshores and mudflats
>   Recommendation: Squaw Creek NWR or Riverlands Demo Area,
>   October-November

___**Sanderling**
>Status: Uncommon migrant
>Habitat: Lakeshores and mudflats
>Recommendation: Riverlands Demo Area, September

___**Semipalmated Sandpiper**
>Status: Common migrant
>Habitat: Lakeshores and mudflats
>Recommendation: Eagle Bluffs C.A., August-September

___**Western Sandpiper**
>Status: Uncommon migrant
>Habitat: Lakeshores and mudflats
>Recommendation: Clarence Cannon NWR or Riverlands Demo Area,
>   August-September

___**Least Sandpiper**
>Status: Common migrant; locally abundant
>Habitat: Lakeshores and wetlands
>Recommendation: Eagle Bluffs C.A. or Riverlands Demo Area,
>   August-September

___**White-rumped Sandpiper**
>Status: Uncommon migrant
>Habitat: Lakeshores and mudflats
>Recommendation: Squaw Creek C.A., May

___**Baird's Sandpiper**
>Status: Rare migrant
>Habitat: Lakeshores and wet fields
>Recommendation: Squaw Creek C.A. or Riverlands Demo Area,
>   August-September

___**Pectoral Sandpiper**
>Status: Uncommon migrant
>Habitat: Wet fields and marshy shores
>Recommendation: Otter Slough C.A. or Mingo NWR, April;
>   Riverlands Demo Area, September

___**Upland Sandpiper**
>Status: Uncommon summer resident in western Missouri
>Habitat: Fields and meadows
>Recommendation: Prairie State Park & vicinity, June

___**Buff-breasted Sandpiper**
Status: Rare migrant
Habitat: Fields and meadows
Recommendation: Riverlands Demo Area, September

GULLS & TERNS

___**Franklin's Gull**
Status: Common migrant; locally abundant
Habitat: Lakes, rivers and marshy grasslands
Recommendation: Squaw Creek NWR or Smithville Lake,
    September-November

___**Bonaparte's Gull**
Status: Uncommon migrant
Habitat: Lakes and rivers
Recommendation: Riverlands Demo Area, April or October

___**Ring-billed Gull**
Status: Common winter resident; locally abundant
Habitat: Lakes and rivers
Recommendation: Riverlands Demo Area, Smithville Lake or
    southwest Great Lakes, winter

___**Herring Gull**
Status: Common winter resident
Habitat: Lakes and rivers
Recommendation: Riverlands Demo Area, winter

___**Glaucous Gull**
Status: Rare winter visitor
Habitat: Lakes and rivers
Recommendation: Riverlands Demo Area, winter

___**Thayer's Gull**
Status: Rare winter visitor
Habitat: Lakes and rivers
Recommendation: Riverlands Demo Area, winter

___**Lesser Black-backed Gull**
Status: Rare but regular winter visitor
Habitat: Lakes and rivers
Recommendation: Riverlands Demo Area, winter

___**Great Black-backed Gull**
> Status: Rare winter visitor
> Habitat: Lakes and rivers
> Recommendation: Riverlands Demo Area, winter

___**Common Tern**
> Status: Uncommon migrant
> Habitat: Lakes and rivers
> Recommendation: Riverlands Demo Area or Smithville Lake,
> April-May or September

___**Forster's Tern**
> Status: Common migrant
> Habitat: Lakes, rivers and wetlands
> Recommendation: Riverlands Demo Area or Smithville Lake,
> April-May or September

___**Least Tern**
> Status: Locally common summer resident in southeast Missouri;
> rare summer visitor on lakes and rivers throughout the State
> Habitat: Lakes and rivers
> Recommendation: Riverlands Demo Area, summer

___**Black Tern**
> Status: Common migrant
> Habitat: Lakes and wetlands; often feed over cropfields
> Recommendation: Ted Shanks C.A. and Clarence Cannon NWR,
> mid-late May; Eagle Bluffs C.A., late August

___**Caspian Tern**
> Status: Uncommon migrant
> Habitat: Lakes and rivers
> Recommendation: Smithville Lake or Eagle Bluffs C.A., September

VULTURES

___**Turkey Vulture**
> Status: Common summer resident; locally abundant; permanent
> resident in southern half of Missouri
> Habitat: Open country with bluffs or woodlands for roosting
> Recommendation: Eagle Bluffs C.A., August-September

___**Black Vulture**
Status: Common summer resident in southern Missouri
Habitat: Open country with bluffs or woodlands for roosting
Recommendation: Mingo NWR, September-October

EAGLES, KITES, HAWKS & OSPREYS

___**Golden Eagle**
Status: Rare winter resident and visitor
Habitat: Open country with bluffs or woodlands for roosting
Recommendation: Squaw Creek NWR, winter

___**Bald Eagle**
Status: Locally common winter resident; more than fifty pair now
        summer and nest in Missouri
Habitat: Lakes and rivers
Recommendation: Squaw Creek NWR, November-December;
        Clarksville Dam, winter. Over 2600 bald eagles now winter
        in Missouri and more than 50 pair nest in the State; nesting
        sites include Ted Shanks C.A., Clarence Cannon NWR,
        Mingo NWR and Riverlands Demonstration Area.

Bald Eagle   (photo by Sherm Spoelstra)

___**Mississippi Kite**
  Status: Uncommon summer resident in southeast Missouri; summer
      visitor north of the Missouri River
  Habitat: Wooded marshes and grasslands
  Recommendation: Mingo NWR, April-September

___**Northern Harrier**
  Status: Common permanent resident
  Habitat: Grasslands, wetlands and cropfields
  Recommendation: Prairie State Park, Eagle Bluffs C.A. or River-
      lands Demo Area, all year

___**Sharp-shinned Hawk**
  Status: Uncommon winter resident; permanent resident in northern
      Missouri
  Habitat: Open woodlands
  Recommendation: Ted Shanks C.A., October-April

___**Cooper's Hawk**
  Status: Uncommon permanent resident
  Habitat: Open woodlands
  Recommendation: Mingo NWR, all year

___**Northern Goshawk**
  Status: Rare winter visitor
  Habitat: Forest and open woodlands
  Recommendation: Swan Lake NWR, winter

___**Red-shouldered Hawk**
  Status: Common permanent resident
  Habitat: Riparian woodlands
  Recommendation: Mingo NWR, all year

___**Broad-winged Hawk**
  Status: Uncommon summer resident
  Habitat: Forest
  Recommendation: Lake of the Ozarks S.P., April-September

___**Red-tailed Hawk**
  Status: Common permanent resident
  Habitat: Open country with nearby woodlands
  Recommendation: Farmlands around Smithville Lake or Little
      Dixie Lake, all year. Common along highways and
      country roads where they often perch on tree limbs.

Red-tailed Hawk

Photo by
  Sherm Spoelstra

___**Swainson's Hawk**
    Status: Uncommon summer resident in western Missouri
    Habitat: Open grasslands
    Recommendation: Prairie State Park, summer

___**Rough-legged Hawk**
    Status: Uncommon winter resident
    Habitat: Open country with nearby woodlands
    Recommendation: Swan Lake NWR, winter

___**Osprey**
    Status: Uncommon migrant
    Habitat: Lakes and rivers
    Recommendation: Schell-Osage C.A. or Smithville Lake, April
        and October

FALCONS

___**American Kestrel**
    Status: Common permanent resident
    Habitat: Open country with trees, wires or poles for perching
    Recommendation: Bradford Farm, winter

___**Merlin**
>Status: Rare winter resident and visitor
>Habitat: Open woodlands
>Recommendation: Swan Lake NWR, winter

___**Prairie Falcon**
>Status: Rare winter resident and visitor
>Habitat: Open grasslands
>Recommendation: Squaw Creek NWR, November-March

___**Peregrine Falcon**
>Status: Uncommon permanent resident
>Habitat: Wetlands with nearby bluffs or trees
>Recommendation: Mingo NWR, Fountain Grove C.A., March-April;
>Riverlands Demo Area, October-December

GROUSE, QUAIL & TURKEY

___**Ruffed Grouse**
>Status: Local permanent populations across Missouri
>Habitat: Forest and open woodlands
>Recommendation: Ted Shanks C.A., October-April

___**Greater Prairie Chicken**
>Status: Local permanent resident in Osage Plains and northern
>Missouri
>Habitat: Tallgrass prairie
>Recommendation: Prairie State Park, April-June

___**Northern Bobwhite**
>Status: Common permanent resident
>Habitat: Open woodlands and brushy grasslands
>Recommendation: Schell-Osage C.A. and Taberville Prairie, all
>year

___**Ring-necked Pheasant**
>Status: Common permanent resident in northwest Missouri; locally
>uncommon in northern half of State
>Habitat: croplands
>Recommendation: Squaw Creek NWR, November-April

___**Wild Turkey**
Status: Common permanent resident
Habitat: Open woodlands and forest clearings
Recommendation: Lake of the Ozarks S.P., Little Dixie Lake C.A.
or Ted Shanks C.A., October-April

DOVES

___**Rock Dove**
Status: Common permanent resident; locally abundant
Habitat: cities and farmlands
Recommendation: Widespread

___**Mourning Dove**
Status: Common permanent resident
Habitat: farmlands, grasslands and open woodlands
Recommendation: Widespread

CUCKOOS & ROADRUNNERS

___**Yellow-billed Cuckoo**
Status: Common summer resident
Habitat: Riparian woodlands
Recommendation: Clarence Cannon NWR, May-September

___**Black-billed Cuckoo**
Status: Uncommon summer resident
Habitat: Riparian woodlands
Recommendation: Mingo NWR, May-September

___**Greater Roadrunner**
Status: Permanent resident in extreme southwest Missouri
Habitat: Brushy grasslands and open woodlands
Recommendation: Henning C.A., summer

OWLS

___Barn Owl
>Status: Rare permanent resident
>Habitat: Farmlands with buildings for roost site
>Recommendation: Mingo NWR, October-April

___Short-eared Owl
>Status: Rare permanent resident in northern and western Missouri;
>uncommon winter resident throughout the State
>Habitat: Open grasslands and wetlands
>Recommendation: Bradford Farm, winter

___Long-eared Owl
>Status: Rare winter resident
>Habitat: Forested areas with nearby fields
>Recommendation: Squaw Creek NWR or Ted Shanks C.A., winter

___Great Horned Owl
>Status: Common permanent resident
>Habitat: Woodlands with adjacent grasslands or marsh
>Recommendation: Swan Lake NWR or Little Dixie Lake area,
>October-April

Great Horned Owls

(photo by Sherm Spoelstra)

___**Barred Owl**
> Status: Common permanent resident
> Habitat: Riparian woodlands
> Recommendation: Mingo NWR, April; Little Bean Marsh, October-
>   November

___**Snowy Owl**
> Status: Rare and erratic winter visitor
> Habitat: Open grasslands
> Recommendation: Swan Lake NWR, winter

___**Eastern Screech Owl**
> Status: Common permanent resident
> Habitat: Forest and woodlots
> Recommendation: Lake of the Ozarks S.P., October-April

___**Northern Saw-whet Owl**
> Status: Rare winter resident
> Habitat: Dense conifers with adjacent meadows
> Recommendation: Squaw Creek NWR, winter

NIGHTJARS & SWIFTS

___**Chuck-will's-widow**
> Status: Common summer resident
> Habitat: Open woodlands
> Recommendation: Prairie State Park, summer

___**Whip-poor-will**
> Status: Common summer resident
> Habitat: Open woodlands
> Recommendation: Prairie State Park, summer

___**Common Nighthawk**
> Status: Common summer resident
> Habitat: Urban areas and open woodlands
> Recommendation: Over cities and towns on calm, summer evenings;
>   especially abundant late August through September

___**Chimney Swift**
> Status: Abundant summer resident
> Habitat: Urban and suburban areas
> Recommendation: Over towns and cities on summer evenings

HUMMINGBIRDS

___Ruby-throated Hummingbird
  Status: Common summer resident
  Habitat: Woodland borders, gardens and urban parks
  Recommendation: Backyard and nature center feeders, Ted Shanks
    C.A. or Clarence Cannon NWR, May-September

KINGFISHERS

___Belted Kingfisher
  Status: Common permanent resident
  Habitat: Riparian woodlands, especially along backwaters of
    lakes and reservoirs
  Recommendation: Swan Lake NWR or Eagle Bluffs C.A., March-
    November

WOODPECKERS

___Red-bellied Woodpecker
  Status: Common permanent resident
  Habitat: Open woodlands
  Recommendation: Widespread

___Northern Flicker
  Status: Common permanent resident
  Habitat: Open woodlands
  Recommendation: Widespread

___Red-headed Woodpecker
  Status: Common but local permanent resident
  Habitat: Riparian woodlands; especially common in drowned
    trees of lake backwaters
  Recommendation: Little Dixie Lake, winter; Schell-Osage C.A.,
    May-June

___Yellow-bellied Sapsucker
  Status: Uncommon winter resident
  Habitat: Forest and woodlots
  Recommendation: Clarence Cannon NWR or Ted Shanks C.A.,
    October-April

Drowned timber offers choice habitat for kingfishers
and red-headed woodpeckers

___**Downy Woodpecker**
　　　Status: Common permanent resident
　　　Habitat: Forest and woodlots
　　　Recommendation: Widespread

___**Hairy Woodpecker**
　　　Status: Common permanent resident
　　　Habitat: Forest and woodlots
　　　Recommendation: Lake of the Ozarks State Park, all year

___**Pileated Woodpecker**
　　　Status: Uncommon permanent resident; locally common
　　　Habitat: Forest
　　　Recommendation: Big Oak Tree State Park and Lake of the Ozarks
　　　　　State Park, all year

KINGBIRDS & FLYCATCHERS

___**Eastern Kingbird**
Status: Common summer resident
Habitat: Riparian woodlands
Recommendation: Eagle Bluffs C.A. or Schell-Osage C.A., May-
September

*Eastern Kingbird
(photo by Sherm
Spoelstra)*

___**Western Kingbird**
Status: Rare summer resident in western Missouri
Habitat: Open grasslands
Recommendation: Prairie State Park, summer

___**Scissor-tailed Flycatcher**
Status: Locally common summer resident in western Missouri
Habitat: Prairie grasslands and open woodlands
Recommendation: Prairie State Park and vicinity, May-September

___**Great Crested Flycatcher**
Status: Common summer resident
Habitat: Open woodlands
Recommendation: Mingo NWR, May-September

___Olive-sided Flycatcher
>   Status: Uncommon migrant; rare summer resident
>   Habitat: Open woodlands
>   Recommendation: Mingo NWR, April-September

___Eastern Wood Pewee
>   Status: Common summer resident
>   Habitat: Forest and woodlots
>   Recommendation: Lake of the Ozarks S.P., May-September

___Eastern Phoebe
>   Status: Common summer resident
>   Habitat: Open woodlands
>   Recommendation: Clarence Cannon NWR, March-May

___Least Flycatcher
>   Status: Common summer resident in western Missouri; uncommon
>   migrant elsewhere
>   Habitat: Open woodlands
>   Recommendation: Prairie State Park, May-September

___Acadian Flycatcher
>   Status: Common summer resident
>   Habitat: Forest, especially near streams
>   Recommendation: Mingo NWR, May-September

___Willow Flycatcher
>   Status: Uncommon summer resident
>   Habitat: Open woodlands and brushy meadows
>   Recommendation: Ted Shanks C.A., May-September

___Alder Flycatcher
>   Status: Uncommon migrant; rare summer visitor
>   Habitat: Riparian woodlands and thickets
>   Recommendation: Squaw Creek NWR or Ted Shanks C.A.,
>   May and September

___Yellow-bellied Flycatcher
>   Status: Rare migrant
>   Habitat: Riparian woodlands
>   Recommendation: Clarence Cannon NWR, May

LARKS

___**Horned Lark**
Status: Common permanent resident
Habitat: Open grasslands and crop fields
Recommendation: Bradford Farm, winter

SWALLOWS

___**Tree Swallow**
Status: Common summer resident
Habitat: Open woodlands, especially near lakes
Recommendation: Ted Shanks C.A., April-May

___**Purple Martin**
Status: Common summer resident
Habitat: Open country with communal houses or nesting cavities
Recommendation: Clarence Cannon NWR or Smithville Lake,
    May-September

___**Bank Swallow**
Status: Locally common summer resident
Habitat: Steep river banks and lakeside cliffs
Recommendation: Clarence Cannon NWR, May-September

___**Northern Rough-winged Swallow**
Status: Uncommon summer resident
Habitat: Streams and rivers; nest under bridges or along banks
Recommendation: Ted Shanks C.A. or Clarence Cannon NWR,
    May-September

___**Cliff Swallow**
Status: Common summer resident
Habitat: Cliffs, riverbanks and bridges in open country
Recommendation: Squaw Creek C.A. or Eagle Bluffs C.A., May-
    September

___**Barn Swallow**
Status: Common summer resident
Habitat: Farmlands and other open areas with buildings or
    bridges for nest sites
Recommendation: Ted Shanks C.A. or Prairie State Park, May-
    September

JAYS & CROWS

___**Blue Jay**
  Status: Abundant permanent resident
  Habitat: Open woodlands and suburbs
  Recommendation: Widespread

___**American Crow**
  Status: Abundant permanent resident
  Habitat: Open country, farmlands and cropfields
  Recommendation: Widespread

___**Fish Crow**
  Status: Common summer resident in southeast Missouri
  Habitat: River valleys
  Recommendation: Big Oak Tree State Park and Mingo NWR,
      April-October

TITMICE & CHICKADEES

___**Tufted Titmouse**
  Status: Common permanent resident
  Habitat: Forest and woodlots
  Recommendation: Little Dixie Lake, winter

___**Black-capped Chickadee**
  Status: Common permanent resident in northwestern 2/3 of Missouri
  Habitat: Forest and open woodlands
  Recommendation: Little Dixie Lake and C.W. Green C.A., winter

___Carolina Chickadee
  Status: Common permanent resident in southeastern 1/3 of Missouri
  Habitat: Forest and open woodlands
  Recommendation: Mingo NWR, April-October

NUTHATCHES & CREEPERS

___**White-breasted Nuthatch**
  Status: Common permanent resident
  Habitat: Forest and open woodlands
  Recommendation: Lake of the Ozarks S.P., October-March

___**Red-breasted Nuthatch**
>   Status: Uncommon winter resident
>   Habitat: Coniferous woodlands
>   Recommendation: Mingo NWR, October-March; feeders in winter

___**Brown Creeper**
>   Status: Common winter resident
>   Habitat: Forest, woodlots and open woodlands
>   Recommendation: Lake of the Ozarks S.P., October-March

WRENS

___**House Wren**
>   Status: Common summer resident
>   Habitat: Immature woodlands, wood margins and suburban areas
>   Recommendation: Widespread

___**Winter Wren**
>   Status: Uncommon migrant: winter resident in southern half of
>   Missouri
>   Habitat: riparian woodlands
>   Recommendation: Mingo NWR, November-March

___**Carolina Wren**
>   Status: Common permanent resident
>   Habitat: Forest undergrowth, wood borders and suburban areas
>   Recommendation: Big Oak Tree State Park, April-May

___**Bewick's Wren**
>   Status: Rare to uncommon permanent resident
>   Habitat: Brushy meadows and wood margins
>   Recommendation: Mingo NWR, April-June

___**Marsh Wren**
>   Status: Uncommon and local summer resident
>   Habitat: Wetlands
>   Recommendation: Riverlands Demo Area or Squaw Creek NWR,
>   April-May

___**Sedge Wren**
>   Status: Locally common summer resident
>   Habitat: Marshlands and wet meadows
>   Recommendation: Ted Shanks C.A. or Clarence Cannon NWR,
>   May-September

KINGLETS & GNATCATCHERS

___Golden-crowned Kinglet
  Status: Uncommon winter resident; locally common
  Habitat: Coniferous woodlands
  Recommendation: Mingo NWR, winter

___Ruby-crowned Kinglet
  Status: Uncommon migrant
  Habitat: Open woodlands, thickets and wood margins
  Recommendation: Lake of the Ozarks S.P., October

___Blue-gray Gnatcatcher
  Status: Common summer resident
  Habitat: Riparian woodlands, thickets and wood margins
  Recommendation: Mingo NWR, April-May

BLUEBIRDS & THRUSHES

___Eastern Bluebird
  Status: Common permanent resident
  Habitat: Wooded meadows and farmlands
  Recommendation: Countryside around Smithville Lake, Eagle
      Bluffs C.A., April-October

Bluebird country

___Wood Thrush
  Status: Common summer resident
  Habitat: Forest
  Recommendation: Lake of the Ozarks S.P., May-September

___**Veery**
>Status: Uncommon migrant
>Habitat: Riparian woodlands and thickets
>Recommendation: Ted Shanks C.A. or Clarence Cannon NWR,
>   May and September

___**Swainson's Thrush**
>Status: Common migrant
>Habitat: Wood margins, thickets, suburban areas
>Recommendation: Eagle Bluffs C.A., May and September

___**Gray-cheeked Thrush**
>Status: Uncommon migrant
>Habitat: Forest and woodlots
>Recommendation: Ted Shanks C.A., May and September

___**Hermit Thrush**
>Status: Uncommon winter resident, primarily in southern half
>   of Missouri
>Habitat: Forest, woodlots and thickets
>Recommendation: Mingo NWR, October-March

___**American Robin**
>Status: Abundant permanent resident
>Habitat: Lawns and fields in summer; woodlands, thickets and berry
>   patches in winter
>Recommendation: Widespread

SHRIKES

___**Loggerhead Shrike**
>Status: Uncommon permanent resident
>Habitat: Brushy grasslands and open woodlands
>Recommmendation: Prairie State Park, June

___**Northern Shrike**
>Status: Rare winter resident in northern Missouri
>Habitat: Brushy grasslands and open woodlands
>Recommendation: Squaw Creek NWR or Swan Lake NWR, winter

CATBIRDS, MOCKINGBIRDS & THRASHERS

___Gray Catbird
>   Status: Common summer resident
>   Habitat: Wood margins and thickets
>   Recommendation: Ted Shanks C.A., May-September

___Northern Mockingbird
>   Status: Common permanent resident; primarily a summer resident
>   in northern Missouri
>   Habitat: Wood margins, thickets and open woodlands
>   Recommendation: Mingo NWR, all year

___Brown Thrasher
>   Status: Common summer resident; permanent resident in southern
>   Missouri
>   Habitat: Undergrowth, thickets and immature woodlands
>   Recommendation: Schell-Osage C.A., May-June

PIPITS

___American Pipit
>   Status: Rare to uncommon migrant
>   Habitat: Fields and meadows, especially near lakes
>   Recommendation: Otter Slough C.A., April; Riveland Demo Area,
>   September-November

WAXWINGS

___Bohemian Waxwing
>   Status: Erratic, rare winter visitor in northern Missouri
>   Habitat: Wood margins and thickets with berry-producing shrubs
>   Recommendation: Squaw Creek NWR, winter

___Cedar Waxwing
>   Status: Erratic permanent resident
>   Habitat: Wood margins, open woodlands and berry patches
>   Recommendation: C.W. Green C.A., October-April
>   See photo next page

*Cedar Waxwing
(photo by Sherm
Spoelstra)*

STARLINGS

___**European Starling**
  Status: Abundant permanent resident
  Habitat: Urban, suburban and rural areas
  Recommendation: Widespread

VIREOS

___**White-eyed Vireo**
  Status: Common summer resident
  Habitat: Wood margins and thickets, especially near streams
  Recommendation: Mingo NWR, May-June

___**Yellow-throated Vireo**
  Status: Uncommon summer resident; locally common
  Habitat: Riparian woodlands
  Recommendation: Mingo NWR or Ted Shanks C.A., May-June

___**Bell's Vireo**
Status: Locally common summer resident
Habitat: Riparian woodlands
Recommendation: Mingo NWR or Taberville Prairie, May-June

___ **Solitary Vireo**
Status: Uncommon migrant
Habitat: Open woodlands and forest margins
Recommendation: Ted Shanks C.A., May and September

___**Red-eyed Vireo**
Status: Common summer resident
Habitat: Forest canopy
Recommendation: Lake of the Ozarks S.P., May-September

___**Warbling Vireo**
Status: Common summer resident
Habitat: Open woodlands
Recommendation: Clarence Cannon NWR or Ted Shanks C.A.,
        May-September

___**Philadelphia Vireo**
Status: Uncommon migrant
Habitat: Open, riparian woodlands
Recommendation: Ted Shanks C.A., May and September

WARBLERS

___**Prothonotary Warbler**
Status: Common summer resident
Habitat: Riparian woodlands
Recommendation: Big Oak Tree S.P. or Schell-Osage C.A.,
        May-June

___**Blue-winged Warbler**
Status: Rare migrant; local summer resident
Habitat: Grassland thickets and immature woodlands
Recommendation: Prairie State Park, June

___**Golden-winged Warbler**
Status: Rare migrant
Habitat: Wood margins and thickets
Recommendation: Mingo NWR, May

___Tennessee Warbler
>   Status: Common migrant
>   Habitat: Open woodlands
>   Recommendation: Ted Shanks C.A., late April-May

___Orange-crowned Warbler
>   Status: Uncommon migrant
>   Habitat: Wood margins and thickets
>   Recommendation: Clarence Cannon NWR, September

___Nashville Warbler
>   Status: Common migrant
>   Habitat: Immature woodlands and thickets
>   Recommendation: Mingo NWR, May

___Northern Parula
>   Status: Common summer resident
>   Habitat: Coniferous or mixed woodlands
>   Recommendation: Ted Shanks C.A., May-June

___Black & White Warbler
>   Status: Common migrant; uncommon summer resident
>   Habitat: Forest and woodlots
>   Recommendation: Ted Shanks C.A., May-June

___Black-throated Blue Warbler
>   Status: Uncommon migrant in Mississippi Valley
>   Habitat: Forest
>   Recommendation: Big Oak Tree State Park, early May

___Cerulean Warbler
>   Status: Uncommon summer resident in eastern Missouri
>   Habitat: Open, riparian woodlands
>   Recommendation: Ted Shanks C.A., May-June

___Blackburnian Warbler
>   Status: Uncommon migrant
>   Habitat: Forest and woodlots
>   Recommendation: Mingo NWR, May

___Chestnut-sided Warbler
>   Status: Uncommon migrant
>   Habitat: Open, immature woodlands
>   Recommendation: Ted Shanks C.A., May and September

___**Cape May Warbler**
Status: Rare migrant
Habitat: Open, coniferous woodlands
Recommendation: Mingo NWR, May

___**Magnolia Warbler**
Status: Common migrant
Habitat: Coniferous woodlands
Recommendation: Ted Shanks C.A., May

___**Yellow-rumped Warbler**
Status: Common winter resident
Habitat: Forest and open woodlands
Recommendation: Little Bean Marsh, October-November

___**Black-throated Green Warbler**
Status: Uncommon migrant
Habitat: Open, coniferous woodlands
Recommendation: Mingo NWR, April-May

___**Yellow-throated Warbler**
Status: Uncommon summer resident
Habitat: Riparian woodlands
Recommendation: Mingo NWR, May

___**Prairie Warbler**
Status: Uncommon summer resident
Habitat: Open woodlands and brushy meadows
Recommendation: Mingo NWR, May

___**Bay-breasted Warbler**
Status: Uncommon migrant
Habitat: Open woodlands and woodlots
Recommendation: Ted Shanks C.A., May

___**Blackpoll Warbler**
Status: Uncommon migrant
Habitat: Open, coniferous woodlands
Recommendation: Ted Shanks C.A., April-May

___**Pine Warbler**
Status: Rare summer resident; rare permanent resident in south-
eastern Missouri
Habitat: Coniferous woodlands
Recommendation: Mingo NWR, April-May

___**Palm Warbler**
>Status: Common migrant
>Habitat: Wetlands, brushy meadows and wood margins
>Recommendation: Ted Shanks C.A., April-May

___**Yellow Warbler**
>Status: Common summer resident
>Habitat: Riparian woodlands
>Recommendation: Ted Shanks C.A., May-June

___**Mourning Warbler**
>Status: Uncommon migrant
>Habitat: Riparian woodlands and thickets
>Recommendation: Mingo NWR, May

___**Connecticut Warbler**
>Status: Rare migrant
>Habitat: Riparian woodlands and thickets
>Recommendation: Ted Shanks C.A., May

___**Kentucky Warbler**
>Status: Common summer resident
>Habitat: Forest undergrowth
>Recommendation: Big Oak Tree State Park, May-September

___**Canada Warbler**
>Status: Uncommon migrant
>Habitat: Forest undergrowth and wood margins
>Recommendation: Clarence Cannon NWR, May

___**Wilson's Warbler**
>Status: Common migrant
>Habitat: Riparian woodlands and thickets
>Recommendation: Ted Shanks C.A., May and September

___**Hooded Warbler**
>Status: Locally common summer resident
>Habitat: Forest undergrowth
>Recommendation: Big Oak Tree State Park, May-September

___**Worm-eating Warbler**
>Status: Uncommon summer resident
>Habitat: Forest undergrowth
>Recommendation: Ted Shanks C.A., May-June

___**Swainson's Warbler**
      Status: Uncommon summer resident in southeast Missouri
      Habitat: Riparian woodlands and thickets; nests in cane
      Recommendation: Big Oak Tree State Park, May-September

*Swainson's warblers nest
at Big Oak Tree State Park*

___**Ovenbird**
      Status: Common migrant; uncommon summer resident
      Habitat: Forest undergrowth
      Recommendation: Lake of the Ozarks S.P. or Mingo NWR,
          May and September

___**Louisiana Waterthrush**
      Status: Uncommon summer resident
      Habitat: Forest undergrowth, especially along streams
      Recommendation: Mingo NWR, May

___**Northern Waterthrush**
      Status: Uncommon migrant
      Habitat: Riparian woodlands and thickets
      Recommendation: Clarence Cannon NWR, April-May

___**Common Yellowthroat**
      Status: Common summer resident
      Habitat: Wetland thickets
      Recommendation: Ted Shanks C.A. or Clarence Cannon NWR, May;
          Eagle Bluffs C.A., August-September

___**Yellow-breasted Chat**
    Status: Common summer resident
    Habitat: Brushy meadows and wood margins
    Recommendation: Prairie State Park, May-June

___**American Redstart**
    Status: Common migrant; uncommon summer resident
    Habitat: Open, immature woodlands
    Recommendation: Mingo NWR, May

GROSBEAKS, BUNTINGS, TOWHEES & SPARROWS

___**Rose-breasted Grosbeak**
    Status: Uncommon summer resident; locally common
    Habitat: Open woodlands and wood margins, especially near
       streams
    Recommendation: Ted Shanks C.A., May-June

___**Northern Cardinal**
    Status: Abundant permanent resident
    Habitat: Thickets, wood margins and immature woodlands
    Recommendation: Widespread

___**Blue Grosbeak**
    Status: Rare to uncommon summer resident
    Habitat: Open, immature woodlands and brushy meadows
    Recommendation: Prairie State Park, June

___**Indigo Bunting**
    Status: Common summer resident
    Habitat: Open woodlands, wood margins and brushy meadows
    Recommendation: Ted Shanks C.A., May-September

___**Painted Bunting**
    Status: Uncommon summer resident in extreme southwest Missouri
       and along southern border of the State
    Habitat: Immature woodlands, roadside thickets and wood
       margins
    Recommendation: Henning C.A., summer

___**Rufous-sided Towhee**
    Status: Common permanent resident; more abundant in summer
    Habitat: Brushy hillsides, wood margins and thickets
    Recommendation: Prairie State Park, June

___**Grasshopper Sparrow**
    Status: Common summer resident
    Habitat: Open grasslands and meadows
    Recommendation: Prairie State Park, June

Prairie State Park is a good place to find
grasshopper and Henslow's sparrows

___**Henslow's Sparrow**
    Status: Locally common summer resident
    Habitat: Meadows, fields and prairie remnants
    Recommendation: Prairie State Park & Taberville Prairie, June

___**LeConte's Sparrow**
    Status: Uncommon migrant; rare, local permanent resident
    Habitat: Wet meadows and marshy thickets
    Recommendation: Ted Shanks C.A., May and September

___**Sharp tailed Sparrow**
    Status: Rare migrant
    Habitat: Wetland thickets
    Recommendation: Ted Shanks C.A. or Riverlands Demo Area,
        September-October

___**Vesper Sparrow**
>Status: Uncommon summer resident in northern and western Missouri;
>>migrant elsewhere
>Habitat: Open grasslands and meadows
>Recommendation: Squaw Creek NWR, April and September

___**Savannah Sparrow**
>Status: Common summer resident; permanent resident in southeast
>>Missouri
>Habitat: Grasslands, meadows and wetlands
>Recommendation: Prairie State Park, June

___**Song Sparrow**
>Status: Common permanent resident
>Habitat: Thickets, especially along streams and in wetlands
>Recommendation: Widespread

___**Lark Sparrow**
>Status: Uncommon summer resident
>Habitat: Brushy meadows and fields
>Recommendation: Ted Shanks C.A., May-June

___**Bachman's Sparrow**
>Status: Rare and local summer resident in southern Missouri
>Habitat: Open coniferous woodlands
>Recommendation: Ted Shanks C.A., May-June

___**American Tree Sparrow**
>Status: Common winter resident
>Habitat: Brushy fields and streamside thickets
>Recommendation: Charles W. Green C.A., winter

___**Field Sparrow**
>Status: Common permanent resident
>Habitat: Weedy fields and open woodlands
>Recommendation: Widespread

___**Chipping Sparrow**
>Status: Common summer resident
>Habitat: Wooded meadows and forest margins
>Recommendation: Mingo NWR or Lake of the Ozarks S.P., May-
>>September

___**Clay-colored Sparrow**
      Status: Rare migrant
      Habitat: Wooded meadows and thickets
      Recommendation: Ted Shanks C.A. or Riverlands Demo Area,
         April-May

___**Dark-eyed Junco**
      Status: Abundant winter resident
      Habitat: Roadsides, thickets and weedy fields; common in
         suburban areas
      Recommendation: Widespread

___**Harris' Sparrow**
      Status: Uncommon winter resident; most common in western
         half of Missouri
      Habitat: Brushy fields and wooded meadows
      Recommendation: Prairie State Park or Squaw Creek NWR, winter

___**White-throated Sparrow**
      Status: Common winter resident
      Habitat: Weedy fields, thickets and suburban yards
      Recommendation: Widespread

___**White-crowned Sparrow**
      Status: Uncommon winter resident; locally common
      Habitat: Wooded meadows and brushlands
      Recommendation: Ted Shanks C.A. or Mingo NWR, October-April

___**Fox Sparrow**
      Status: Uncommon winter resident
      Habitat: Streamside thickets and forest undergrowth
      Recommendation: Ted Shanks C.A. or Riverlands Demo Area,
         November-March

___**Lincoln's Sparrow**
      Status: Uncommon migrant; rare winter resident
      Habitat: Riparian thickets and wetlands
      Recommendation: C.W. Green C.A. or Ted Shanks C.A., March-
         April or October-November

___**Swamp Sparrow**
      Status: Uncommon winter resident; locally common
      Habitat: Wetland thickets
      Recommendation: C.W. Green C.A. or Little Dixie Lake C.A.,
         November-March

___Smith's Longspur
Status: Rare winter resident; locally uncommon
Habitat: Open grasslands and fields
Recommendation: Riverlands Demo Area, winter

___Lapland Longspur
Status: Uncommon and erratic winter resident
Habitat: Open grasslands and fields
Recommendation: Bradford Farm, winter

Bradford farm:
longspur habitat

___Snow Bunting
Status: Rare and erratic winter visitor
Habitat: Open grasslands and fields
Recommendation: Riverlands Demo Area, winter

___Dickcissel
Status: Common summer resident
Habitat: Open grasslands and wooded meadows
Recommendation: Prairie State Park or Eagle Bluffs C.A.,
    May-June

BOBOLINKS, MEADOWLARKS & BLACKBIRDS

___Bobolink
Status: Locally common summer resident in northern Missouri;
    migrant elsewhere
Habitat: Meadows and grassy fields
Recommendation: Ted Shanks C.A., May-June

___**Eastern Meadowlark**
>Status: Common permanent resident
>Habitat: Open grasslands and fields
>Recommendation: Bradford Farm or Prairie S.P., all year

___**Western Meadowlark**
>Status: Uncommon permanent resident in western Missouri
>Habitat: Open grasslands and fields
>Recommendation: Prairie State Park or Squaw Creek NWR, June-
>September

___**Yellow-headed Blackbird**
>Status: Locally common summer resident, especially in northern
>and western Missouri
>Habitat: Wetlands
>Recommendation: Squaw Creek NWR, April-June

___**Red-winged Blackbird**
>Status: Abundant permanent resident; huge flocks in fall-winter
>Habitat: Wetlands and farmlands
>Recommendation: Widespread

___**Rusty Blackbird**
>Status: Uncommon winter resident; locally common
>Habitat: Riparian woodlands
>Recommendation: Mingo NWR, winter

___**Brewer's Blackbird**
>Status: Rare to uncommon winter resident
>Habitat: Fields and farmlands
>Recommendation: Mingo NWR, winter

___**Brown-headed Cowbird**
>Status: Common permanent resident
>Habitat: Open woodlands and wood margins; common in suburban
>areas
>Recommendation: Widespread

___**Common Grackle**
>Status: Abundant permanent resident
>Habitat: Fields, farmlands and open woodlands; common in
>residential areas
>Recommendation: Widespread

___**Great-tailed Grackle**
    Status: Rare summer visitor in western Missouri
    Habitat: Fields, open woodlands and wetlands
    Recommendation: Squaw Creek NWR, August-September

ORIOLES

___**Orchard Oriole**
    Status: Common summer resident
    Habitat: Open woodlands and wood margins
    Recommendation: Ted Shanks C.A., May-September

___**Northern Oriole**
    Status: Common summer resident
    Habitat: Open woodlands and wood margins; especially common
        along streams
    Recommendation: Clarence Cannon NWR, May-September

TANAGERS

___**Scarlet Tanager**
    Status: Common summer resident
    Habitat: Forest
    Recommendation: Mingo NWR or Ted Shanks C.A., May

___**Summer Tanager**
    Status: Uncommon summer resident
    Habitat: Open woodlands and wood margins, especially near
        streams and lakes
    Recommendation: Ted Shanks C.A., May-June

WEAVERS

___**House Sparrow**
    Status: Abundant permanent resident
    Habitat: Urban, suburban and rural areas
    Recommendation: Widespread

___**Eurasian Tree Sparrow**
    Status: Common permanent resident in Greater St. Louis
    Habitat: Urban parks, suburban areas and farmlands
    Recommendation: St. Louis parklands or Riverlands Demo Area,
        all year

FINCHES & CROSSBILLS

___**Pine Siskin**
> Status: Uncommon winter resident
> Habitat: Open, coniferous woodlands
> Recommendation: Check backyard feeders in March-April;
>> Ted Shanks C.A., March-April

___**American Goldfinch**
> Status: Common permanent resident; locally abundant
> Habitat: Weedy fields and roadsides; common in suburban areas
> Recommendation: Widespread

___**Red Crossbill**
> Status: Rare and erratic winter visitor
> Habitat: Coniferous woodlands
> Recommendation: Squaw Creek NWR, winter

___**White-winged Crossbill**
> Status: Rare and erratic winter visitor
> Habitat: Coniferous woodlands
> Recommendation: Ted Shanks C.A., winter

___**Common Redpoll**
> Status: Rare and erratic winter visitor
> Habitat: Brushy fields and meadows
> Recommendation: Squaw Creek NWR or Swan Lake NWR, winter

___**Purple Finch**
> Status: Common winter resident
> Habitat: Open, coniferous woodlands
> Recommendation: Check feeders December-March; Lake of the
>> Ozarks State Park or Mingo NWR, winter

___**House Finch**
> Status: Abundant permanent resident
> Habitat: Open woodlands; common in suburban areas
> Recommendation: Widespread

___**Evening Grosbeak**
> Status: Rare and erratic winter visitor
> Habitat: Coniferous woodlands
> Recommendation: Check feeders, December-March; Mingo NWR
>> or Clarence Cannon NWR, winter

APPENDIX

MISSOURI CONSERVATION ORGANIZATIONS

The following is a partial list of conservation organizations that are working to protect Missouri's natural heritage. Your support for their efforts will help to ensure the future welfare of the State's wild lands which are vital to the health of our resident and migrant wildlife.

Audubon Society of Missouri
1001 Walnut, Suite 200, Columbia, Missouri 65201
573-442-2583
Missouri Bird Alert: 573-445-9115
www.audubon.org/chapter/mo/mo

Columbia Audubon Society
Box 1331, Columbia, Missouri 65203

Burroughs Audubon Society (Greater Kansas City)
www.burroughs.org
Bird Alert Hotline: 913-342-2473

Greater Ozarks Audubon Society (Springfield Area)
www.geocities.com/greaterozarksaudubon

River Bluffs Audubon Society (Jefferson City)
www.rbas.org

St. Louis Audubon Society
Box 220227, Kirkwood, Missouri 63122
314-822-6595
www.stlouisaudubon.org
Bird Alert Hotline: 314-935-8432

Center for Plant Conservation
www.mobot.org/CPC/welcome.html

Conservation Federation of Missouri
728 W. Main, Jefferson City, Missouri 65101
573-634-2322, 800-575-2322
www.confedmo.com

Eastern National Forests Interpretive Association
4549 State Rd. H, Fulton, Missouri 65251

Forest Releaf of Missouri
4207 Lindell Blvd., St. Louis, Missouri 63108
314-533-5323
www.moreleaf.org

Katy Trail Coalition
1001 E. Walnut, #300, Columbia, Missouri 65201
573-443-1602

Mark Twain National Forest
401 Fairgrounds Rd., Rolla, Missouri 65401
314-364-4621

Missouri Coalition for the Environment
6267 Delmar, 2E, St. Louis, Missouri 63130
314-727-0600
moenviron@aol.com

Missouri Conservation Heritage Foundation
www.outreach.missouri.edu/mowin/mchf

Missouri Department of Conservation
Box 180, Jefferson City, Missouri 65102
www.conservation.state.mo.us

Missouri Department of Natural Resources
Box 176, Jefferson City, Missouri 65102
800-334-6946
www.dnr.state.mo.us

Missouri Native Plant Society
Box 20073, St. Louis, Missouri 63144
314-894-9021
www.missouri.edu/~umo_herb/monps

Missouri Parks Association
Box 1811, Jefferson City, Missouri 65102
Membership: Box 42, Fulton, Missouri 65251

Missouri Prairie Foundation
Box 200, Columbia, Missouri 65202
573-442-5842

Missouri Trails & Streams Association
>Box 1478, Ballwin, Missouri 63021
>314-532-4742

The Nature Conservancy of Missouri
>2800 South Brentwood Blvd., St. Louis, Missouri 63144
>314-968-1105
>www.nature.org/wherewework/northamerica/states/mo

Sierra Club
>**Ozark Chapter**
>>1007 N. College, Suite 1, Columbia, Missouri 65201
>>573-815-9250
>>email: ozark.chapter@sierraclub.org
>>www.missouri.sierraclub.org

>**Osage Group (Columbia)**
>>contact via Ozark Chapter website

>**Eastern Missouri Group**
>>314-644-0890
>>missouri.sierraclub.org/emg/index.asp

>**Thomas Hart Benton Group**
>>Box 32727, Kansas City, Missouri 64171-5727
>>www.kcwebs.org/sierraclub

>**Trail of Tears Group (Cape Girardeau)**
>>contact via Ozark Chapter website

BIBLIOGRAPHY

FIELD GUIDES

Bull, John and John Farrand, Jr., **The Audubon Society Field Guide to North American Birds: Eastern Region**, Alfred A. Knopf, New York, 1977

Peterson, Roger Tory, **A Field Guide to the Birds East of the Rockies**, Houghton Mifflin Company, Boston, 1980 and later editions

Robbins, Chandler S. et al., **Birds of North America, A Guide to Field Identification**, Golden Press, New York, 1966 and subsequent editions

Scott, Shirley L., Editor, **Field Guide to the Birds of North America**, National Geographic Society, Washington, D.C., 1983, 1987

REGIONAL GUIDES

Jacobs, Brad and James D. Wilson, **Missouri Breeding Bird Atlas, 1986-1992**, Natural History Series, No. 6, Missouri Department of Conservation, Jefferson City, 1997

Palmer, Kay (compiler), **A Guide to the Birding Areas of Missouri**, Audubon Society of Missouri, 1993

Robbins, Mark B. and David A. Easterla, **Birds of Missouri, Their Distribution and Abundance**, University of Missouri Press, Columbia and London, 1992

Zimmerman, John L. and Sebastian T. Patti, illustrated by Robert M. Mengel, **A Guide to Bird Finding in Kansas and Western Missouri**, University Press of Kansas, 1988

BIRD LISTS

Animal Checklist for Prairie State Park, Missouri Department of Natural Resources, Prairie State Park, Box 97, Liberal, Missouri 64762

Birds of the Smithville Lake Area, compiled by the Burroughs Audubon Society of Greater Kansas City, published by the U.S. Corps of Engineers

Birds of Squaw Creek National Wildlife Refuge, revised 5/96 by David A. Easterla, Squaw Creek N.W.R., Box 158, Mound City, Missouri 64470 816-442-3187

Birds of Ted Shanks Wildlife Area, Missouri Department of Conservation, Ted Shanks Wildlife Area Headquarters, Box 13, Ashburn, Missouri 63433

Checklist of Birds for the Riverlands Environmental Demonstration Area Dedicated to memory of Jack Van Benthuysen U.S. Corps of Engineers, Riverlands Area Office, 301 Riverlands Way, West Alton, Missouri 63386; 636-899-2600

Clarence Cannon National Wildlife Refuge Bird Checklist, Clarence Cannon N.W.R., Box 88, Annada, Missouri 63330, 573-847-2333

Lake of the Ozarks State Park Animal Checklist, Missouri Department of Natural Resources, Lake of the Ozarks State Park, Kaiser, Missouri 65047

Mingo National Wildlife Refuge Bird Checklist, Mingo N.W.R., 24279 State Highway 51, Puxico, Missouri 63960, 573-222-3589

Swan Lake National Wildlife Refuge Bird Checklist, Swan Lake N.W.R. Box 68, Sumner, Missouri 64681, 816-856-3323

BIRDING WEBSITES

Birding.com - Where to Bird in Missouri: www.birding.com/wheretobird/missouri.asp

Missouri Birding Hotspots: www.camacdonald.com/birding/usmissouri

Missouri Online Bird Clubs: birding.about.com/cs/clubsmissouri

Virtual Birder.com - Rare Bird Alert Hotlines www.virtualbirder.com/vbirder/realbirds/rbas/mo

INDEX